Everyman, I will go with thee,
and be thy guide

Four Metaphysical Poets

Selected and edited by DOUGLAS BROOKS-DAVIES

EVERYMAN
J. M. Dent · London

For Mary, for the past and future

Selection, introduction and other critical apparatus
© J. M. Dent 1997

All rights reserved

J. M. Dent
Orion Publishing Group
Orion House
5 Upper St Martin's Lane,
London WC2H 9EA

Typeset by Deltatype Ltd, Birkenhead, Merseyside
Printed and Great Britain by
The Guernsey Press Co. Ltd., Guernsey, C. I.

This book if bound as a paperback is subject to the
condition that it may not be issued on loan or otherwise
except in its original binding.

British Library Cataloguing-in-Publication
Data is available upon request.

ISBN 0 460 87857 3

Contents

George Herbert

Andrew Marvell

Henry Vaughan

Note on the Authors and Editor

JOHN DONNE, born in 1572 into a Catholic family, proceeded from Oxford to Lincoln's Inn, sailed with Essex to sack Cadiz (1596), and in 1597 entered the service of the Lord Keeper of England, Sir Thomas Egerton, though his secret marriage to Egerton's niece led to his disgrace. Having converted from Catholicism, he was ordained in 1615 and elected Dean of St Paul's (1621). He died in 1631; his *Poems* appeared in 1633.

GEORGE HERBERT, born in 1593 into a prominent Montgomery family, attended Westminster School, proceeding to Trinity College, Cambridge, where he became a fellow, subsequently being elected the University's Praelector in Rhetoric and then Public Orator. He was ordained deacon by July 1626, though he did not become a parish priest until 1630. He died in 1633; *The Temple* appeared posthumously the same year.

ANDREW MARVELL, born in 1621, son of a Yorkshire vicar, went from Hull Grammar School to Trinity College, Cambridge in 1633. After continental travel from 1642–7, he returned to England, and gained the notice of Cromwell's Commander-in-Chief, Fairfax. He was appointed Latin Secretary to the Council of State in 1657, and in 1659 was elected M.P. for Hull. He died in 1678; the poems for which he is now most famous were published in 1681.

HENRY VAUGHAN, Silurist (from the tribe which anciently inhabited south-east Wales), was born in Breconshire in 1621, twin brother to Thomas, and spent most of his life there. Physician and poet, he married around 1646 and was much influenced by the mystical occultism of the time (as was his twin brother Thomas, the Hermetic philosopher and alchemist, who died in 1666). His prose works include *Hermetical Physic* (1655). His *Silex Scintillans* ('Sparkling Flint'; 1650, enlarged 1655), was inspired by Herbert's *The Temple*. He died in 1695 and is buried in Llansantffraed churchyard.

DOUGLAS BROOKS-DAVIES was born in London and educated at

Merchant Taylors' School, Crosby, and Brasenose College, Oxford. Formerly Senior Lecturer in English Literature at the University of Manchester, he is now an Honorary Research fellow there, and a freelance scholar. His publications include *The Mercurian Monarch* (Manchester University Press, 1983); *Silver Poets of the Sixteenth Century* (Dent, 1992, 1994); *Spenser: Selected Shorter Poems* (Longman, 1995); a modernised Spenser, *The Fairy Queen* (Dent, 1996) and *Robert Herrick* and *Alexander Pope* (Everyman's Poetry, 1996).

Chronology of the Poets' Lives

Year	Life
1572	John Donne born, London; son of John (Catholic merchant) and Elizabeth, Catholic, daughter of John Heywood and grand-niece of Sir Thomas More
1576	Death of father; mother marries Dr John Syminges
1577	Death of Elizabeth Donne (sister)
1581	November, death of sisters Mary and Katherine Donne
1584	October, matriculates from Hart Hall, Oxford with Henry Donne (brother)
1588	Death of stepfather
1588–91	At Cambridge; then abroad
1590–1	Mother marries Richard Rainsford, a Catholic
1591(?)	Enters Thavies Inn
1592	Enters Lincoln's Inn
1593	3 April, George Herbert born, Montgomery, Wales, 5th son of Richard and Magdalen. Death of Henry Donne in prison, accused of harbouring Catholic priest
1596	Donne on Cadiz expedition under Essex and Ralegh. Death of Herbert's father
1597	Donne on expedition to Azores
1597–8	Donne enters service of Sir Thomas Egerton, Lord Keeper of England
1601	Donne enters parliament as M.P. for Brackley, Northants; December, secret marriage to Ann More, daughter of Egerton's brother-in-law, Sir George More

Chronology of their Times

Year	Literary Context	Historical Events
1572	Ronsard, *La Franciade*	Paris: St Bartholomew Massacre of French Protestants
1576		Frobisher annexes Frobisher Bay
1577	Holinshed, *Chronicles*	Frobisher's second voyage
1581	Tasso, *Gerusalemme Liberata*	Act against Catholics; Anjou courts Elizabeth I
1584		Expulsion of Jesuits; William of Orange assassinated
1588	William Morgan, Welsh translation of Bible	Defeat of the Spanish Armada
1590	Marlowe, *Tamburlaine* Spenser, *Faerie Queene* Books 1–3 Sidney, *Arcadia*	
1591	Harington, translation of Ariosto, *Orlando Furioso*	Death of Spanish mystic St John of the Cross; Trinity College, Dublin founded
1592	Marlowe, *Edward II, Dr Faustus*	Presbyterianism established in Scotland
1593	Shakespeare, *Richard III* Marlowe dies	Act against Jesuits
1596	Spenser, *Faerie Queene*, Books 4–6	English (led by Essex) attack Cadiz

Year	*Life*
1602	Donne confesses marriage; dismissed by Egerton
1605	Donne in France and Italy; birth of son, George. Herbert at Westminster School
1606	Donne family moves to Mitcham
1607	Donne urged by Thomas Morton, Dean of Gloucester, to be ordained; says he is unworthy
1608	Donne fails to get secretaryship in Ireland; birth of daughter Lucy. Herbert's mother marries Sir John Danvers
1609	Herbert matriculates at Trinity College, Cambridge
1610	Donne: *Pseudo-Martyr* published; honorary Oxford M.A.
1611	Donne: *Ignatius his Conclave; First Anniversary*
1612	Donne on continent with Sir Robert Drury
1613	December, Donne seriously ill
1615	23 January, Donne ordained at St Paul's Cathedral; James I's chaplain; March: king compels Cambridge to make Donne honorary DD
1616	Donne appointed Divinity Reader at Lincoln's Inn. Herbert elected major fellow of Trinity
1617	August, death of Ann Donne (wife) in childbirth
1618	Herbert appointed Reader in Rhetoric at Cambridge
1619	Donne to Germany with Viscount Doncaster
1620	21 January, Herbert appointed Public Orator at Cambridge (until 1628)

Year	Literary Context	Historical Events
1603	Jonson, *Sejanus*	Death of Elizabeth I; James VI succeeds as James I and grants tolerance to Catholics
1605	Jonson, *Volpone* acted (published 1607) Shakespeare, *King Lear*	Gunpowder Plot
1607	Shakespeare, *Anthony and Cleopatra*	English settlement in Virginia; Tyrone flees to Rome; land in Ulster given to English and Scottish settlers
1608	Birth of John Milton	Telescope invented by Lippersheim
1610	Jonson, *The Alchemist*	Bishops fully restored in Scotland
1611	Authorised Version of Bible	Kepler invents astronomical telescope
1613	Shakespeare, *Henry VIII*	Marriage of Princess Elizabeth to Elector Palatine
1616	Folio edition of Jonson's works Death of Shakespeare, Cervantes	Richelieu becomes French Secretary of State
1617	Middleton and Rowley, *Fair Quarrel*	Pocahontas at court; dismissal of Richelieu
1618		Bacon Lord Chancellor; Ralegh executed; Thirty Years' War
1619	Death of Nicholas Hilliard, Samuel Daniel	Villiers created Marquess of Buckingham
1620	Bacon, *Novum organum*	Pilgrim Fathers leave Plymouth in *Mayflower*

Year	Life
1621	31 March, Andrew Marvell born, Yorkshire, son of the Reverend Andrew and Anne. Henry Vaughan and twin brother Thomas born, Newton-upon-Usk, Breconshire, to Thomas and Denise. Donne installed as Dean of St Paul's
1624	Herbert M.P. for Montgomery. Marvell family move to Hull
1626	Herbert, already a deacon, made prebendary attached to Lincoln Cathedral
1627	Death of Herbert's mother; Donne preaches the funeral sermon
1628	Vaughan's brother William probably born
1629	Herbert marries stepfather's cousin, Jane Danvers
1630	Herbert inducted at Bemerton Church, near Salisbury; 19 September, ordained priest
1631	January, death of Donne's mother; Donne poses for portrait in his shroud; 31 March, death of Donne
1633	1 March, death of Herbert; Herbert: *The Temple*; *Poems by J[ohn] D[onne]*, with *Elegies on the Author's Death*. Marvell leaves Hull Grammar School for Trinity College, Cambridge
1638	April, death of Marvell's mother. Thomas (and possibly Henry) Vaughan at Oxford
1639	Marvell receives B.A.; briefly converts to Catholicism
1640	Walton's *Life of Dr John Donne*. Herbert's *Outlandish Proverbs*. Vaughan in London reading law (?)
1641	Death of Marvell's father

Year	Literary Context	Historical Events
1621	Burton, *Anatomy of Melancholy*	
1624	Middeton, *Game at Chess*	Virginia a Crown colony; Dutch found New Amsterdam
1625	Massinger's *A New Way to Pay Old Debts*	Death of James I; Charles I succeeds, marries French Catholic Henrietta Maria
1626	Sandys, Ovid translation Death of Bacon	Irish College founded at Rome
1627	Bacon, *New Atlantis*	Propaganda College founded at Rome
1628		Harvey reveals double circulation of blood; Buckingham assassinated; Taj Mahal built
1629		Parliament dissolved by Charles I; Laud censors press
1630	Drayton, *Muses' Elizium*	Birth of Charles II; drainage of fens; 'Great Migration' to New England; death of Kepler
1631		English colonisation of Leeward islands
1633	Spenser, *View of Ireland*	Laud appointed Archbishop of Canterbury
1634	Death of Chapman	First levy of ship-money
1637	Milton, *Comus*	Scots resist new Prayer Book; trial of John Hampden
1640	Death of Rubens	First session of Long Parliament; Stafford impeached
1641	Death of Van Dyck	Stafford executed; Protestants massacred in Ulster

Year	Life
1642–7	Marvell on continent; writes some verses. Vaughan: *Poems with the Tenth Satire of Juvenal . . .* (1646)
1648	July, death of William Vaughan
1650	Marvell: *An Horatian Ode*; at Nun Appleton with Fairfax (until (?) July 1652). Vaughan: *Silex Scintillans, I*
1651	Vaughan: *Olor Iscanus*
1652	*Herbert's Remains* (contains *A Priest to the Temple*)
1653	Marvell tutor to William Dutton (later Cromwell's ward)
1655	Vaughan: *Hermetical Physic; Silex Scintillans, I and II*
1656	Marvell in France with Dutton
1657	September, Marvell appointed Latin Secretary to Council of State. Vaughan: *The Chemist's Key*
1658	Death of Vaughan's father, Thomas

Year	Literary Context	Historical Events
1642	Browne, *Religio medici* Denham, *Cooper's Hill*	Civil War begins; theatres closed until Restoration; death of Galileo
1643	Milton, *Doctrine and Discipline of Divorce*	Defeat of Hampden (royalist victory); Solemn League and Covenant between Parliament and Scots; bishops abolished
1644	Milton, *Areopagitica*	Defeat of Royalists at Marston Moor; Louis xiv King of France
1645	Waller, *Poems* Milton, *Poems*	Defeat of Royalists at Naseby; Laud executed; Fairfax creates New Model Army; Prayer Book abolished
1647	Cowley, *The Mistress* Cleveland, *Poems*	Scots sell captured Charles I to Parliament; escapes to Isle of Wight
1648	Herrick, *Hesperides*	Second Civil War; Pride's Purge; Thirty Years War ends
1649	Milton, *Eikonoklastes* Lovelace, *Lucasta*	30 January Charles I executed; Commonwealth declared
1650	Taylor, *Holy Living*	Scots defeated at Dunbar; Edinburgh Castle surrenders
1651	Hobbes, *Leviathan*	Charles II crowned at Scone; defeated by Cromwell at Battle of Worcester; Charles to France
1652	Ashmole, *Theatrum Chemicum Britannicum*	England fights Dutch; Royalists pardoned
1653	Walton, *Complete Angler*	Cromwell dissolves Long Parliament; made Lord Protector
1655	Junius, *Caedmon's Genesis*	Proclamation on religious liberty
1656	Cowley, *Poems*	Toleration of Jews; second Protectorate Parliament
1657	King, *Poems*	Cromwell declines kingship; Quakers protected
1658		Cromwell dies; son Richard succeeds

Year	Life
1659	Marvell elected M.P. for Hull
1662–3	Marvell in Holland
1663–5	Marvell in Russia, Sweden, Denmark as Secretary to Earl of Carlisle
1666	27 February, death of Vaughan's twin brother, Thomas
1671–78	Marvell: various writings, including *The Rehearsal Transprosed* (1672) and *An Account of the Growth of Popery and Arbitrary Government* (anonymously, 1677)
1678	16 August, death of Marvell
1681	Marvell: *Miscellaneous Poems*
1695	23 April, death of Vaughan

Year	Literary Context	Historical Events
1659		End of Protectorate
1660	Dryden, *Astraea Redux*	Restoration of Charles II
1665		Plague of London
1666	Dryden, *Annus Mirabilis*	Fire of London
1667	Milton, *Paradise Lost*	
1671	Milton, *Paradise Regained, Samson Agonistes*	
1673	Dryden, *Amboyna*	Test Act excludes Catholics from offices under Crown
1674	Wycherley, *The Country Wife, The Plain Dealer* Death of Milton	England withdraws from Dutch war
1678	Bunyan, *Pilgrim's Progress*	Titus Oates alleges Catholic conspiracy; Catholics excluded from Parliament
1681	Dryden, *Absalom and Achitophel*	
1685		Death of Charles II; accession of Catholic James II; Duke of Monmouth's rebellion; 'Bloody Assizes'
1688		'Glorious Revolution': William of Orange lands at Torbay; James flees to France
1689		Coronation of William III and Mary II
1695	Congreve, *Love for Love*	Press censorship ends in England

Introduction

The metaphysical poets inhabited a world of darkness. For Donne it was the tortured darkness of the hell and damnation he fights off in his Holy Sonnets, the gloom of the sick-room, the shadowy fragmentation of an imperfect world fallen (with him) from grace, the enclosed beds in which he postures with whichever woman he imagines himself to be accompanied by at the time. Everything is reduced: his and his mistress's blood within the jet walls of a flea; the universe to a bedchamber ('The Good Morrow'); geography – celestial and terrestrial – to the confined space of the invalid ('Hymn to God'). Writing 'The Apparition' – perhaps by candlelight – Donne imagines the woman who has scorned him to be lonely and loveless, a 'sick taper' (that is, dying), shivering with the other-worldly gleam of a 'quicksilver sweat' (has he poisoned her?). Or the woman whom he has adored and has now either left him or died is, in 'A Nocturnal', imagined as St Lucy – patron saint of sight and light, whose feast day, 13 December, was so near the winter solstice that Donne commemorates her in one of the most terrible hymns to blackness and negation that has ever been penned. It is at once an image of the world's death (as in *An Anatomy of the World. The First Anniversary*) and an experiment in anti-alchemy culminating, not in the philosophers' stone which yields gold and spiritual illumination, but in 'absence, darkness, death', 'a quintessence even from nothingness'. As the narrating poet becomes one with his subject, his mind numbs, and the external world assumes a hallucinatory aura of otherness – as it does so often in Donne's poems. The Donne who, born into an intensely Catholic family, rejected his forbidden faith for worldly preferment and lost that preferment through an ill-judged marriage, recovered enough (after poverty and the claustrophobia of an over-large family in a Mitcham cottage) to become ordained, a royal chaplain, and Dean of St Paul's, but never felt secure. His true faith always beckoned him, accusing him with the image of family martyrs whose precedent he had betrayed. The darkness was real: if Roman Catholicism was the true faith, his soul was condemned. Fierce play-acting was one answer; so he produced the poetic equivalent of getting drunk the night before one was hanged. The play-acting became deadly serious when, dressed in his funeral shroud, he posed for his portrait and died shortly after.

Donne wrote a characteristically witty mystical mathematical squib on primroses at Montgomery Castle, home of the Herberts ('The Primrose'). He also preached at the burial of Herbert's mother, whom he had known for many years. Despite these cross-weavings, the two poets had little in common. Herbert achieved wordly success with a spectacular public career at Cambridge (the university which, forced by King James I, had reluctantly bestowed an honorary Doctorate of Divinity on Donne), abandoning public life for the less exposed demands of parish work after ordination (though many of his poems were written before this). He had no problems with his faith: he was an Anglican, soaked in liturgy and ecclesiastical architecture (but you would not know from reading Herbert that his faith's churches were inhabited by the ghosts of generations of faithful Roman Catholics whose icons, paint and gilding had been despoiled at the Reformation), and he was, above all (and this is what marks out any Protestant poet of the time from his Catholic fellows), deeply intimate with the Bible. Donne rejected the imagistic codes and posturings of the love verse of his contemporaries, offering instead an outrageous and shocking roughness and macho realism which, nevertheless, could not forget the tug of the spiritual life and the patterns of the forbidden faith ('The Canonisation', 'A Nocturnal'); Herbert, on the other hand, *saw through* love poetry. It wasn't relevant (Jordan (1)); it had profaned divine icons ('The Altar' rescues the unhewn altar of Exodus 20:25 for the pure faith of Anglicanism from the repellent idolatry of the love poets who wrote pattern poems in the shape of altars). Like Donne, Herbert isn't a poet of outdoors either. With him, we sweep rooms; gaze at church floors; read spiritual destiny in the iconography of tombs. But whereas Donne reduces vast cosmic spaces to claustrophobia, Herbert expands little things: sweeping is working for God, reminding ourselves of the dusty mortality He sent Christ to redeem and purify; a collar is at once an image of restraint (on priest, on layman), outraged anger (choler) at the impossible demands of the spiritual life, and a noose which loosens into the parental embrace of a father of rare and tear-jerking gentleness.

*

The lives of Marvell and Vaughan didn't intersect but they were in
various ways parallel. Born in the same year – 1621 – both lived
through the Civil War and were formed by it. Marvell, a Yorkshire-
man who spent much of his life in his home county, flirted with
Roman Catholicism and royalism before finally throwing in his lot
with the Puritan republic; Vaughan (about whose life we know
little) was born in Breconshire, lived most of his life there, spoke
Welsh, may have gone to Oxford, may have been a physician, and
was a staunch royalist. Like Milton (whom he knew well) and
many republicans, Marvell was haunted by the idea of the lost
paradise of Genesis which it was the function of the republic to
restore. Nearly all his poetry is about paradise: Puritan exiles under
Charles I and Archbishop Laud seeking a promised land find it in
the God-given paradisal temple of the Bermudas (Marvell met John
Oxenbridge, who had been just such an exile, at Eton); the Mower –
your average human being bearing with him the constant
reminder that all flesh is as grass – rails against modern horticul-
ture as a perversion of the primal garden's integrity, or – like the
narrator of 'The Garden' – jestingly recalls the perfection of a world
before Eve and her destructive daughter Juliana. The Mower
remains, nevertheless, earthbound in a fallen landscape, whereas
the narrator of 'The Garden' and *Upon Appleton House* liberate
themselves from 'the body's vest' ('The Garden') into a weightless
vocal flight (like a counter-tenor floating in the free spaces of the
head-voice) that leads beyond confinement – of language, gender,
time – into the infinite garden-greenness of the mind, confined
though it be within the cranium.

Worried about duty and public obligation (he accompanied
Fairfax to Nun Appleton after the General had resigned as
Commander-in-Chief of Cromwell's New Model army), Marvell
writes about escape but – like Donne – is riddled with guilt. Paradise
may eventually become political reality – the attaining of the New
Jerusalem in England by the parliamentary forces – but to
anticipate it in the imagination seems like an evasion. And so (*Upon
Appleton House*) the flooding of the fields becomes a reminder of the
Flood of Genesis 6–9 and therefore God's punishment for sin and his
redemption of mankind and the obligation to fight – politically – for
right; the fallen oak symbolises the executed king, realising anxiety
about the rightness of that appalling act, and so on.

If Marvell's light is, in the end, dimmed by trees and green gloom and reduced to the wan incandescence of glow-worms, Vaughan's brilliantly illuminates the immediate landscape of his homeland and, simultaneously, the world beyond. Vaughan is that unusual thing in this period, a genuine landscape poet; but he is also a Platonist mystic who sees in earth's forms and creatures a shadowy anticipation of heaven's brightness. Celebrating outdoor detail for itself – rocks, water, flowers – and winning us over with an enviable conversational ease ('I walked the other day'), he turns his poems rapidly into meditative exercises, exemplary readings in what mediaeval and later divines called the book of nature. But the clue to this poet is loss. His beloved younger brother, William, died aged twenty in 1648, and his death (miming in the personal world the defeat of the king in the political world) precipitated in Vaughan an anguished elegiac quest which resulted in some of the century's best poetry. Soaked in poems and phrases from Herbert's *The Temple*, he reworked Herbert into forlornness, uncertainty and nostalgia underpinned by absolute certainty. 'Vanity of Spirit' is typical in placing him in a landscape that, read over-curiously by myopic, fallen man, turns, dream-like, into a fractured and inscrutable hieroglyphic. It is St Paul's dark glass of 1 Corinthians 13:12; it is also the most moving image of desolation in literature until Keats's overthrown Saturn in *The Fall of Hyperion* (1.319–26).

Sometimes, as I have said, the world is brighter; but it is never as bright as the lost world of childhood ('Childhood'; 'The Retreat'). Vaughan 'dreams of paradise and light' ('Cock crowing'), but his favourite biblical image is that of the midnight bridegroom and the untrimmed lamps of Matthew 25, and for him even a cockerel – a triumphantly solar bird in the mystical symbolism of the time – contains only a few seeds of a greater, divine, light ('Cock crowing').

But what of the umbrella label 'metaphysical'? As a critical term it is hotly disputed, though still generally accepted as a description of the poetic output of Donne, Herbert, Marvell and Vaughan (the main exemplars) along with that of Carew, Cleveland, Cowley, Crashaw, and a limited number of their contemporaries. The term was first used in its modern sense by Dr Johnson (*Life of Cowley*, 1779), though Dryden had, a century earlier, accused Donne of 'affect[ing] the metaphysics, not only in his satires, but in his amorous verses, where nature only should reign' (*Discourse of the Original ... of Satire*, 1692). For Johnson the metaphysicals (exemplified by Cowley) endeavoured to 'show their learning' at the expense of all else; were witty in 'discover[ing] occult resemblances in things apparently unlike'; and were writers of intellect whose 'courtship was devoid of fondness and their lamentation of sorrow'. The term was gradually taken up until, with Herbert Grierson's *Metaphysical Lyrics and Poems of the Seventeenth Century* (1921), we get what, in effect, remains the standard definition of the metaphysical manner: 'passionate, paradoxical argument, touched with humour and learned imagery . . . the sudden roar of passion in bold and felicitous image'. T. S. Eliot, reviewing Grierson, invented the notion of a unified sensibility to explain the metaphysicals' ability to coin imagery from apparently disparate areas of experience (all things were then coherent in a way they aren't now; the celebrated 'metaphysical conceit', although it has its roots in earlier poetic practice, is the supreme manifestation of the identification of thought with feeling). To Grierson's list we may add colloquialisms, epigrammatic tenseness, metrical ingenuity, compression of argument – and a delight in riddling that is forever teasing and fending off an imminent, grinningly hungry Death. The poetry of the four major metaphysicals represented in this volume is also noteworthy for its confrontation of truly metaphysical issues – human aspiration, passion, folly and ignorance seen in the light of God, the universe and what mankind makes of the problem of being. But then, aren't those the concerns of all great poetry? The metaphysicals, when writing at their best, are beyond labels, and the term itself is, perhaps, shorthand of a not particularly useful kind.

DOUGLAS BROOKS-DAVIES

Four Metaphysical Poets

JOHN DONNE

from Songs and Sonnets

The Apparition

When by thy scorn, O murderess, I am dead,
And that thou think'st thee free
From all solicitation from me,
Then shall my ghost come to thy bed,
And thee, feigned vestal, in worse arms shall see.
Then thy sick taper will begin to wink,
And he, whose thou art then, being tired before,
Will, if thou stir, or pinch to wake him, think
       Thou call'st for more,
And in false sleep will from thee shrink;
And then, poor aspen wretch, neglected thou,   10
Bathed in a cold quicksilver sweat, wilt lie,
      A verier ghost than I.
What I will say I will not tell thee now,
Lest that preserve thee; and, since my love is spent,
I'd rather thou should'st painfully repent
Than, by my threatenings, rest still innocent.

The Canonisation

For God's sake hold your tongue, and let me love;
    Or chide my palsy, or my gout;
My five grey hairs, or ruined fortune, flout;
    With wealth your state, your mind with arts improve;
        Take you a course; get you a place;
        Observe His Honour, or His Grace;
And the king's real, or his stampèd, face,
    Contemplate: what you will, approve,
    So you will let me love.

Alas, alas, who's injured by my love?   10
    What merchants' ships have my sighs drowned?
Who says my tears have overflowed his ground?
    When did my colds a forward spring remove?
        When did the heats which my veins fill
        Add one more to the plaguey bill?
Soldiers find wars, and lawyers find out still
    Litigious men which quarrels move,
    Though she and I do love.

Call us what you will, we are made such by love:
    Call her one, me another, fly –   20
We're tapers, too, and at our own cost die,
    And we in us find the eagle and the dove.
    The phoenix riddle hath more wit
        By us: we two, being one, are it;
So, to one neutral thing, both sexes fit.
    We die and rise the same, and prove
    Mysterious by this love.

We can die by it, if not live by love,
    And, if unfit for tombs and hearse
Our legend be, it will be fit for verse;   30
    And if no piece of chronicle we prove,
        We'll build in sonnets pretty rooms:

As well a well-wrought urn becomes
The greatest ashes as half-acre tombs,
   And by these hymns all shall approve
   Us canonised for love,

And thus invoke us: 'You, whom reverend love
   Made one another's hermitage;
You, to whom love was peace that now is rage;
   Who did the whole world's soul contract, and drove   40
      Into the glasses of your eyes
      (So made such mirrors, and such spies,
That they did all to you epitomise)
   Countries, towns, courts: beg from above
   A pattern of your love!'

The Dream

Dear love, for nothing less than thee
Would I have broke this happy dream –
         It was a theme
For reason, much too strong for fantasy;
Therefore thou waked'st me wisely; yet
My dream thou brok'st not, but continued'st it.
Thou art so true that thoughts of thee suffice
To make dreams truths, and fables histories.
Enter these arms; for since thou thought'st it best
Not to dream all my dream, let's act the rest.   10

As lightning, or a taper's light,
Thine eyes, and not thy noise, waked me;
         Yet I thought thee
(For thou loved'st truth) an angel, at first sight.
But when I saw thou saw'st my heart,
And knew'st my thoughts, beyond an angel's art;
When thou knew'st what I dreamt, when thou knew'st when

Excess of joy would wake me, and cam'st then,
I must confess it could not choose but be
Profane to think thee anything but thee.   20

Coming and staying showed thee, thee;
But rising makes me doubt that now
          Thou art not thou.
That love is weak where fear's as strong as he:
'Tis not all spirit, pure and brave,
If mixture it of fear, shame, honour have.
Perchance, as torches which must ready be,
Men light and put out, so thou deal'st with me:
Thou cam'st to kindle, goèst to come. Then I
Will dream that hope again – but else, would die.   30

The Flea

Mark but this flea, and mark in this
How little that which thou deniest me is:
Me it sucked first, and now sucks thee,
And in this flea our two bloods mingled be.
Confess it, this cannot be said
A sin, a shame, or loss of maidenhead;
     Yet this enjoys before it woo
     And, pampered, swells with one blood made of two –
     And this, alas, is more than we would do.

Oh stay – three lives in one flea spare,   10
Where we almost – nay, more than – married are.
This flea is you and I, and this
Our marriage bed, and marriage temple, is.
Though parents grudge, and you, we're met
And cloistered in these living walls of jet.
     Though use make you apt to kill me,
     Let not to this self-murder added be,
     And sacrilege: three sins in killing three.

Cruel and sudden, hast thou since
Purpled thy nail in blood of innocence? 20
In what could this flea guilty be
Except in that drop which it sucked from thee?
Yet thou triumph'st, and say'st that thou
Find'st not thyself, nor me, the weaker now.
    'Tis true. Then learn how false fears be:
    Just so much honour, when thou yield'st to me,
    Will waste, as this flea's death took life from thee.

The Good Morrow

I wonder, by my troth, what thou and I
    Did till we loved? Were we not weaned till then,
But sucked on country pleasures, childishly?
    Or snorted we in the seven sleepers' den?
'Twas so; but this, all pleasure's fancies be:
If ever any beauty I did see
Which I desired, and got, 'twas but a dream of thee.

And now, good morrow to our waking souls,
    Which watch not one another out of fear;
For love all love of other sights controls, 10
    And makes one little room an everywhere.
Let sea-discoverers to new worlds have gone;
Let maps to others, worlds on worlds have shown:
Let us possess one world: each hath one, and is one.

My face in thine eye, thine in mine appears,
    And true plain hearts do in the faces rest:
Where can we find two better hemispheres
    Without sharp north, without declining west?
Whatever dies was not mixed equally:
If our two loves be one, or, thou and I 20
Love so alike that none do slacken, none can die.

Love's Alchemy

Some, that have deeper digged love's mine than I,
Say where his centric happiness doth lie.
      I have loved, and got, and told,
But should I love, get, tell till I were old,
I should not find that hidden mystery.
      Oh, 'tis imposture all;
And as no chemic yet the elixir got,
      But glorifies his pregnant pot
      If by the way to him befall
Some odoriferous thing, or medicinal,   10
    So lovers dream a rich and long delight,
    But get a winter-seeming summer's night.

Our ease, our thrift, our honour, and our day
Shall we, for this vain bubble's shadow, pay?
      Ends love in this, that my man
Can be as happy as I can, if he can
Endure the short scorn of a bridegroom's play?
      That loving wretch that swears
'Tis not the bodies marry but the minds,
      Which he in her angelic finds,   20
      Would swear as justly that he hears,
In that day's rude, hoarse minstrelsy, the spheres.
    Hope not for mind in women: at their best
    Sweetness and wit, they're but mummy, possessed.

Love's Growth

I scarce believe my love to be as pure
    As I had thought it was,
    Because it doth endure
Vicissitude, and season, as the grass.
Methinks I lied all winter when I swore

My love was infinite, if spring make it more.
But if this medicine – love – which cures all sorrow
With more, not only be no quintessence,
But mixed of all stuffs, paining soul, or sense,
And of the sun his working vigour borrow,   10
Love's not so pure and abstract as they use
To say which have no mistress but their muse;
But, as all else, being elemented, too,
Love sometimes would contèmplate, sometimes do.

As yet not greater, but more eminent,
   Love by the spring is grown,
    As, in the firmament,
Stars by the sun are not enlarged, but shown.
Gentle love deeds, as blossoms on a bough.
From love's awakened root do bud out now.   20
If, as in water stirred, more circles be
Produced by one, love such additions take:
Those, like so many spheres, but one heaven make,
For they are all concentric unto thee.
And though each spring do add to love new heat
(As princes do in time of action get
New taxes, and remit them not in peace),
No winter shall abate the spring's increase.

A Nocturnal upon St Lucy's Day, being the Shortest Day

'Tis the year's midnight, and it is the day's,
Lucy's, who scarce seven hours herself unmasks;
   The sun is spent, and now his flasks
    Send forth light squibs, no constant rays;
     The world's whole sap is sunk:
The general balm the hydroptic earth hath drunk,
Whither, as to the bed's feet, life is shrunk,

Dead, and interred. Yet all these seem to laugh
Compared with me, who am their epitaph.

Study me, then, you who shall lovers be   10
At the next world (that is, at the next spring);
    For I am every dead thing,
    In whom Love wrought new alchemy.
      For his art did express
A quintessence even from nothingness,
From dull privations, and lean emptiness:
He ruined me, and I am rebegot
Of absence, darkness, death – things which are not.

All others from all things draw all that's good –
Life, soul, form, spirit – whence they being have.   20
    I, by love's limbeck, am the grave
    Of all that's nothing. Oft a flood
      Have we two wept, and so
Drowned the whole world, us two; oft we did grow
To be two chaoses, when we did show
Care to aught else; and often absences
Withdrew our souls, and made us carcasses.

But I am by her death (which word wrongs her)
Of the first nothing the elixir grown.
    Were I a man, that I were one   30
    I needs must know; I should prefer,
      If I were any beast,
Some ends, some means. Yet plants, yea stones detest
And love; all, all some properties invest:
If I an ordinary nothing were,
As shadow, a light and body must be here.

But I am none, nor will my sun renew.
You lovers – for whose sake the lesser sun
    At this time to the Goat is run   40
    To fetch new lust and give it you –
      Enjoy your summer all:
Since she enjoys her long night's festival,
Let me prepare towards her, and let me call

This hour her vigil and her eve, since this
Both the year's and the day's deep midnight is.

The Primrose

Upon this primrose hill –
Where, if heaven would distil
A shower of rain, each several drop might go
To his own primrose, and grow manna so;
And where their form and their infinity
Make a terrestrial galaxy,
As the small stars do in the sky –
I walk to find a true love, and I see
That 'tis not a mere woman that is she,
But must or more, or less, than woman be.   10

Yet know I not which flower
I wish – a six, or four;
For should my true love less than woman be,
She were scarce anything; and then, should she
Be more than woman, she would get above
All thoughts of sex, and think to move
My heart to study her, not to love.
Both these were monsters. Since there must reside
Falsehood in woman, I could more abide
She were by Art than Nature falsified.   20

Live, primrose, then, and thrive
With thy true number, five;
And women, whom this flower doth represent,
With this mysterious number be content.
Ten is the farthest number; if half ten
Belong unto each woman, then
Each woman may take half us men.

Or, if this will not serve their turn, since all
Numbers are odd or even, and they fall
First into this, five, women may take us all.   30

The Relic

When my grave is broke up again
Some second guest to entertain
(For graves have learned that womanhead
To be to more than one a bed),
          And he that digs it spies
A bracelet of bright hair about the bone,
          Will he not let us alone,
And think that there a loving couple lies
Who thought that this device might be some way
To make their souls, at the last, busy day,   10
Meet at this grave, and make a little stay?

If this fall in a time, or land,
Where misdevotion doth command,
Then he that digs us up will bring
Us to the bishop and the king
          To make us relics. Then
Thou shalt be a Mary Magdalen, and I
          A something else thereby.
All women shall adore us, and some men;
And since at such time miracles are sought,   20
I would have that age by this paper taught
What miracles we harmless lovers wrought.

First, we loved well and faithfully,
Yet knew not what we loved, nor why:
Difference of sex no more we knew

Than our guardian angels do.
    Coming and going we
Perchance might kiss, but not between those meals;
    Our hands ne'er touched the seals
Which Nature, injured by late law, sets free.   30
These miracles we did; but now, alas,
All measure and all language I should pass
Should I tell what a miracle she was.

Song

Go, and catch a falling star,
    Get with child a mandrake root,
Tell me where all past years are,
    Or who cleft the devil's foot;
Teach me to hear mermaids singing,
Or to keep off Envy's stinging,
        And find
        What wind
Serves to advance an honest mind.

If thou be'st born to strange sights,   10
    Things invisible to see,
Ride ten thousand days and nights
    Till age snow white hairs on thee:
Thou, when thou return'st, wilt tell me
All strange wonders that befell thee,
        And swear
        Nowhere
Lives a woman true, and fair.

If thou find'st one, let me know —
    Such a pilgrimage were sweet;   20
Yet do not: I would not go,
    Though at next door we might meet.
Though she were true when you met her,

And last till you write your letter,
        Yet she
        Will be
False, ere I come, to two or three.

Song

Sweetest love, I do not go
    For weariness of thee,
Nor in hope the world can show
    A fitter love for me;
        But since that I
Must die at last, 'tis best
To use myself in jest
    Thus by feigned deaths to die.

Yesternight the sun went hence,
    And yet 'tis here today:
He hath no desire nor sense,
    Nor half so short a way.
        Then fear not me,
But believe that I shall make
Speedier journeys, since I take
    More wings and spurs than he.

Oh, how feeble is man's power
    That, if good fortune fall,
Cannot add another hour,
    Nor a lost hour recall!
        But, come bad chance,
And we join to it our strength,
And we teach it art and length
    Itself o'er us to advance.

When thou sigh'st, thou sigh'st not wind,
    But sigh'st my soul away.

10

20

When thou weep'st, unkindly kind,
  My life's blood doth decay.
    It cannot be
That thou lov'st me, as thou say'st,
If in thine my life thou waste:
    Thou art the best of me.

  Let not my divining heart
    Forethink me any ill:
Destiny may take thy part,
  And may thy tears fulfil;
    But think that we
Are but turned aside to sleep:
They who one another keep
    Alive ne'er parted be.

The Sun Rising

  Busy old fool, unruly Sun,
    Why dost thou thus
Through windows and through curtains call on us?
Must to thy motions lovers' seasons run?
    Saucy, pedantic wretch, go chide
      Late schoolboys and sour 'prentices;
  Go tell court-huntsmen that the king will ride;
  Call country ants to harvest offices:
Love, all alike, no season knows, nor clime,
Nor hours, days, months, which are the rags of Time.

    Thy beams so reverend and strong
      Why should'st thou think?
I could eclipse them with a wink,
But that I would not lose her sight so long.
    If her eyes have not blinded thine,
      Look, and, tomorrow late, tell me
  Whether both th'Indias of spice and mine

Be where thou left'st them, or lie here with me.
Ask for those kings whom thou saw'st yesterday,
And thou shalt hear, all here in one bed lay.   20

　　She's all states, and all princes, I:
　　　　Nothing else is.
Princes do but play us: compared to this,
All honour's mimic, all wealth, alchemy.
　　Thou, Sun, art half as happy as we
　　　　In that the world's contracted thus:
　　Thine age asks ease; and since thy duties be
　　To warm the world, that's done in warming us.
Shine here to us, and thou art everywhere:
This bed thy centre is, and these walls, thy sphere.   30

The Undertaking

　　I have done one braver thing
　　　　Than all the Worthies did;
　　And yet a braver thence doth spring,
　　　　Which is, to keep that hid.

　　It were but madness now to impart
　　　　The skill of specular stone,
　　When he which can have learned the art
　　　　To cut it, can find none.

　　So, if I now should utter this,
　　　　Others (because no more   10
　　Such stuff to work upon there is)
　　　　Would love but as before.

　　But he who loveliness within
　　　　Hath found, all outward loathes,
　　For he who colour loves, and skin,
　　　　Loves but their oldest clothes.

If, as I have, you also do
   Virtue attired in woman see,
And dare love that, and say so, too,
   And forget the he and she;   20

And if this love, though placèd so,
   From profane men you hide,
Which will no faith on this bestow
   (Or, if they do, deride):

Then you have done a braver thing
   Than all the Worthies did,
And a braver thence will spring –
   Which is, to keep that hid.

A Valediction: forbidding Mourning

As virtuous men pass mildly away,
   And whisper to their souls to go,
Whilst some of their sad friends do say
   'The breath goes now', and some say 'no':

So let us melt, and make no noise,
   No tear-floods nor sigh-tempests move:
'Twere profanation of our joys
   To tell the laity our love.

Moving of the earth brings harms and fears –
   Men reckon what it did and meant;   10
But trepidation of the spheres –
   Though greater far – is innocent.

Dull sublunary lovers' love
   (Whose soul is sense) cannot admit
Absence because it doth remove
   Those things which elemented it;

But we, by a love so much refined
    That we ourselves know not what it is,
Inter-assurèd of the mind,
    Care less eyes, lips and hands to miss.   20

Our two souls, therefore, which are one,
    Though I must go, endure not yet
A breach but an expansion –
    Like gold to airy thinness beat.

If they be two, they are two so
    As stiff twin compasses are two –
Thy soul, the fixed foot, makes no show
    To move, but doth if th'other do.

And, though it in the centre sit,
    Yet, when th'other far doth roam,   30
It leans, and hearkens after it,
    And grows erect as that comes home.

Such wilt thou be to me, who must,
    Like th'other foot, obliquely run:
Thy firmness makes my circle just,
    And makes me end where I begun.

Woman's Constancy

Now that thou has loved me one whole day,
Tomorrow, when thou leav'st, what wilt thou say?
Wilt thou then antedate some new-made vow,
    Or say that now
We are not just those persons which we were?
Or, that oaths made in reverential fear
Of Love and his wrath any may forswear?

Or, as true deaths true marriages untie,
So lovers' contracts (images or those)
Bind but till sleep – death's image – them unloose?   10
          Or – your own ends to justify –
For having purposed change and falsehood, you
Can have no way but falsehood to be true?
Vain lunatic – against these scapes I could
          Dispute and conquer, if I would;
          Which I disdain to do,
For, by tomorrow, I may think so too.

from **An Anatomy of the World. The First Anniversary**

(LINES 205–46)

And new philosophy calls all in doubt:
The element of fire is quite put out;
The sun is lost, and the earth, and no man's wit
Can well direct him where to look for it.
And freely men confess that this world's spent:
When, in the planets and the firmament,   210
They seek so many new, they see that this
Is crumbled out again to his atomies.
'Tis all in pieces, all coherence gone,
All just supply and all relation:
Prince, subject, father, son, are things forgot,
For every man alone thinks he hath got
To be a phoenix, and that then can be
None of that kind of which he is, but he.
This is the world's condition now, and now
She that should all parts to reunion bow –   220
She that had all magnetic force alone
To draw and fasten sundered parts in one;
She whom wise Nature had invented then

When she observed that every sort of men
Did in their voyage in this world's sea stray,
And needed a new compass for their way;
She that was best, and first original
Of all fair copies, and the general
Steward to Fate; she whose rich eyes and breast
Gilt the West Indies and perfumed the East;   230
Whose having breathed in this world did bestow
Spice on those isles and bade them still smell so,
And that rich Indie which doth gold inter
Is but as single money coined from her:
She, to whom this world must itself refer
As suburbs, or the microcosm, of her –
She – she is dead; she's dead. When thou know'st this,
Thou know'st how lame a cripple this world is,
And learn'st thus much by our anatomy:
That this world's general sickness doth not lie   240
In any humour or one certain part,
But, as thou sawest it rotten at the heart,
Thou seest a hectic fever hath got hold
Of the whole substance, not to be controlled,
And that thou hast but one way: not to admit
The world's infection; to be none of it.

from Divine Meditations
[Holy Sonnets]

SONNET 5

I am a little world made cunningly
Of elements and an angelic sprite,
But black sin hath betrayed to endless night
My world's both parts, and (oh) both parts must die.
You which beyond that heaven which was most high
Have found new spheres, and of new lands can write,

Pour new seas in mine eyes that so I might
Drown my world with my weeping earnestly,
Or wash it if it must be drowned no more.
But, oh, it must be burnt! Alas, the fire   10
Of lust and envy have burnt it heretofore,
And made it fouler: let their flames retire,
And burn me, O Lord, with a fiery zeal
Of thee and thy house, which doth in eating heal.

SONNET 6

This is my play's last scene: here heavens appoint
My pilgrimage's last mile, and my race –
Idly, yet quickly, run – hath this last pace,
My span's last inch, my minute's latest point,
And gluttonous Death will instantly unjoint
My body and my soul, and I shall sleep a space.
But my ever-waking part shall see that face
Whose fear already shakes my every joint:
Then, as my soul to heaven (her first seat) takes flight,
And earth-born body in the earth shall dwell,   10
So, fall, my sins – that all may have their right –
To where they're bred (and would press me) – to hell.
Impute me righteous, thus purged of evil,
For thus I leave the world, the flesh, and devil.

SONNET 7

At the round earth's imagined corners blow
Your trumpets, angels, and arise, arise
From death you numberless infinities
Of souls, and to your scattered bodies go –
All whom the flood did, and fire shall, o'erthrow;
All whom war, dearth, age, argues, tyrannies,
Despair, law, chance hath slain; and you, whose eyes
Shall behold God, and never taste death's woe.
But let them sleep, Lord, and me mourn a space;
For if, above all these, my sins abound,   10

'Tis late to ask abundance of thy grace
When we are there: here, on this lowly ground,
Teach me how to repent; for that's as good
As if thou hadst sealed my pardon with thy blood.

SONNET 9

If poisonous minerals, and if that tree
Whose fruit threw death on else-immortal us,
If lecherous goats, if serpents envious
Cannot be damned, alas, why should I be?
Why should intent or reason, born in me,
Make sins, else equal, in me more heinous?
And, mercy being easy and glorious
To God in his stern wrath, why threatens he?
But who am I that dare dispute with thee,
O God? Oh, of thine only worthy blood,   10
And my tears, make a heavenly Lethean flood,
And drown in it my sins' black memory.
That thou remember them some claim as debt:
I think it mercy if thou wilt forget.

SONNET 10

Death, be not proud, though some have callèd thee
Mighty and dreadful, for thou art not so;
For those whom thou think'st thou dost overthrow
Die not, poor Death – nor yet canst thou kill me.
From rest and sleep – which but thy pictures be –
Much pleasure; then, from thee, much more must flow,
And soonest our best men with thee do go,
Rest of their bones, and soul's delivery.
Thou art slave to Fate, Chance, kings, and desperate men,
And dost with poison, war, and sickness dwell;   10
And poppy, or charms, can make us sleep as well,

And better, than thy stroke. Why swell'st thou, then?
One short sleep past, we wake eternally,
And death shall be no more: Death, thou shalt die.

SONNET 13

What if this present were the world's last night?
Mark in my heart, O soul (where thou dost dwell)
The picture of Christ crucified, and tell
Whether that countenance can thee affright:
Tears in his eyes quench the amazing light,
Blood fills his frowns, which from his pierced head fell;
And can that tongue adjudge thee unto hell
Which prayed forgiveness for his foes' fierce spite?
No, no. But, as in my idolatry
I said to all my profane mistresses,   10
'Beauty, of pity; foulness only is
A sign of rigour'; so I say unto thee:
'To wicked spirits are horrid shapes assigned;
This beauteous form assures a piteous mind.'

SONNET 14

Batter my heart, three-personed God; for you
As yet but knock, breathe, shine, and seek to mend:
That I may rise, and stand, o'erthrow me, and bend
Your force to break, blow, burn, and make me new.
I, like an usurped town, to another due,
Labour to admit you; but, oh, to no end.
Reason, your viceroy in me, should defend,
But is captived, and proves weak or untrue:
Yet dearly I'll love you, and would be loved fain,
But am betrothed unto your enemy.   10
Divorce me; untie, or break, that knot again;
Take me to you; imprison me; for I,

Except you enthral me, never shall be free,
Nor ever chaste, except you ravish me.

SONNET 17

Since she whom I loved hath paid her last debt
To Nature, and to hers and my good is dead,
And her soul early into heaven ravishèd,
Wholly in heavenly things my mind is set.
Here the admiring her my mind did whet
To seek thee, God: so streams do show the head.
But, though I have found thee, and thou my thirst hast fed,
A holy, thirsty dropsy melts me yet.
But why should I beg more love when as thou
Dost woo my soul for hers, offering all thine,   10
And dost not only fear lest I allow
My love to saints and angels, things divine,
But in thy tender jealousy dost doubt
Lest the world, flesh – yea, devil – put thee out.

A Hymn to Christ, at the Author's last going into Germany

In what torn ship so ever I embark,
That ship shall be the emblem of thy ark;
What sea so ever swallow me, that flood
Shall be to me an emblem of thy blood:
Though thou with clouds of anger do disguise
Thy face, yet, through that mask, I know those eyes,
    Which, though they turn away sometimes,
        They never will despise.

I sacrifice this island unto thee,
And all whom I loved there, and who loved me: 10

When I have put our seas 'twixt them and me,
Put thou thy sea betwixt my sins and thee.
As the tree's sap doth seek the root below
In winter, in my winter now I go,
    Where none but thee, the eternal root
      Of true love, I may know.

Nor thou nor thy religion dost control
The amorousness of an harmonious soul,
But thou would'st have that love thyself. As thou
Art jealous, Lord, so I am jealous now: 20
Thou lov'st not till, from loving more, thou free
My soul: whoever gives, takes liberty.
    Oh, if thou car'st not whom I love,
      Alas, thou lov'st not me.

Seal, then, this bill of my divorce to all
On whom those fainter beams of love did fall:
Marry those loves which, in youth, scattered be
On fame, wit, hopes, false mistresses, to thee.
Churches are best for prayer that have least light:
To see God only, I go out of sight;   30
    And to scape stormy days I choose
      An everlasting night.

Hymn to God, my God, in my Sickness

Since I am coming to that holy room
    Where, with thy choir of saints, for evermore
I shall be made thy music, as I come
    I tune the instrument here at the door
    And, what I must do then, think here before.

Whilst my physicians by their love are grown
    Cosmographers, and I their map, who lie
Flat on his bed, that by them may be shown

That this is my south-west discovery,
  Per fretum febris, by these straits to die,   10

I joy that in these straits I see my west;
  For, though their currents yield return to none,
What shall my west hurt me? As west and east
  In all flat maps (and I am one) are one,
  So death doth touch the resurrection.

Is the Pacific sea my home? Or are
  The eastern riches? Is Jerusalem?
Anyan, and Magellan, and Gibraltar,
  All straits, and none but straits, are ways to them,
  Whether where Japhet dwelt, or Cham, or Shem.   20

We think that paradise and Calvary,
  Christ's cross, and Adam's tree, stood in one place:
Look, Lord, and find both Adams met in me:
  As the first Adam's sweat surrounds my face,
  May the last Adam's blood my soul embrace.

So, in his purple wrapped, receive me, Lord;
  By these his thorns give me his other crown;
And as to others' souls I preached thy word,
  Be this my text, my sermon to mine own:
  Therefore that he may raise, the Lord throws down.   30

GEORGE HERBERT

from **The Temple** (1633)

Superliminare

Thou, whom the former precepts have
Sprinkled, and taught how to behave
Thyself in church: approach, and taste
The church's mystical repast.

Avoid profaneness; come not here:
Nothing but holy, pure and clear,
Or that which groaneth to be so,
May at his peril further go.

Aaron

Holiness on the head,
Light and perfections on the breast,
Harmonious bells below, raising the dead
To lead them unto life and rest:
Thus are true Aarons dressed.

Profaneness in my head,
Defects and darkness in my breast,

A noise of passions ringing me for dead
   Unto a place where is no rest:
      Poor priest, thus am I dressed.   10

      Only another head
   I have, another heart and breast,
Another music, making live, not dead,
   Without whom I could have no rest:
      In him I am well dressed.

      Christ is my only head,
   My alone only heart and breast,
My only music, striking me even dead
   That to the old man I may rest,
      And be in him new dressed.   20

      So, holy in my head,
   Perfect and light in my dear breast,
My doctrine tuned by Christ (who is not dead,
   But lives in me while I do rest) –
      Come, people, Aaron's dressed.

The Altar

A broken altar, Lord, thy servant rears,
Made of a heart, and cemented with tears,
  Whose parts are as thy hand did frame:
  No workman's tool hath touched the same.
      A   heart   alone
      Is such a stone –
      As   nothing, but
      Thy power doth cut.
      Wherefore each part

Of my hard heart
Meets in this frame
To praise thy name
That, if I chance to hold my peace,
These stones to praise thee may not cease.
Oh, let thy blessed sacrifice be mine,
And sanctify this altar to be thine.

10

$$\textit{Ana} - \begin{cases} \textsf{MARY} \\ \textsf{ARMY} \end{cases} \textit{gram}$$

How well her name an army doth present,
In whom the Lord of hosts did pitch his tent!

The Church Floor

Mark you the floor? That square and speckled stone,
Which looks so firm and strong,
Is Patience;

And the other, black and grave, wherewith each one
Is chequered all along,
Humility.

The gentle rising which, on either hand,
Leads to the choir above,
Is Confidence;

But the sweet cement which, in one sure band,
Ties the whole frame, is Love
And Charity.

10

      Hither sometimes Sin steals, and stains
      The marble's neat and curious veins:
But all is cleansed when the marble weeps.
      Sometimes Death, puffing at the door,
      Blows all the dust about the floor:
But, while he thinks to spoil the room, he sweeps.
      Blessed be the architect, whose art
      Could build so strong in a weak heart.   20

Church Monuments

While that my soul repairs to her devotion,
Here I entomb my flesh, that it betimes
May take acquaintance of this heap of dust,
To which the blast of Death's incessant motion,
Fed with the exhalation of our crimes,
Drives all at last. Therefore I gladly trust

My body to this school, that it may learn
To spell his elements, and find his birth
Written in dusty heraldry and lines;
Which dissolution sure doth best discern,   10
Comparing dust with dust, and earth with earth.
These laugh at jet and marble, put for signs

To sever the good fellowships of dust,
And spoil the meeting. What shall point out them
When they shall bow, and kneel, and fall down flat
To kiss those heaps which now they have in trust?
Dear flesh, while I do pray, learn here thy stem
And true descent that, when thou shalt grow fat

And wanton in thy cravings, thou may'st know
That flesh is but the glass which holds the dust   20
That measures all our time, which also shall
Be crumbled into dust. Mark, here below,

How tame these ashes are, how free from lust,
That thou may'st fit thyself against thy fall.

The Collar

I struck the board, and cried, 'No more:
               I will abroad.
What! Shall I ever sigh and pine?
My lines and life are free – free as the road,
    Loose as the wind, as large as store:
          Shall I be still in suit?
Have I no harvest but a thorn
To let me blood and not restore
What I have lost with cordial fruit?
               Sure, there was wine,   10
    Before my sighs did dry it; there was corn
    Before my tears did drown it.
  Is the year only lost to me?
     Have I no bays to crown it?
No flowers, no garlands gay? All blasted?
          All wasted?
  Not so, my heart; but there is fruit,
          And thou hast hands.
    Recover all thy sigh-blown age
On double pleasures: leave thy cold dispute   20
Of what is fit, and not forsake thy cage,
         Thy rope of sands,
Which petty thoughts have made, and made to thee
  Good cable, to enforce and draw,
        And be thy law,
  While thou did'st wink and would'st not see.
        Away: take heed:
        I will abroad.
Call in thy death's head there: tie up thy fears.

He that forbears   30
To suit and serve his need
Deserves his load.'
But, as I raved and grew more fierce and wild
At every word,
Methoughts I heard one calling 'Child';
And I replied, 'My Lord.'

Denial

When my devotions could not pierce
Thy silent ears,
Then was my heart broken, as was my verse:
My breast was full of fears
And disorder;

My bent thoughts, like a brittle bow,
Did fly asunder:
Each took has way – some would to pleasures go,
Some to wars and thunder
Of alarms.   10

As good go anywhere, they say,
As to benumb
Both knees and heart in crying night and day
'Come, come, my God, O come',
But no hearing.

Oh that thou should'st give dust a tongue
To cry to thee,
And then not hear it crying! All day long
My heart was in my knee,
But no hearing.   20

Therefore my soul lay out of sight,
                    Untuned, unstrung:
My feeble spirit, unable to look right,
                    Like a nipped blossom hung
                                Discontented.

Oh cheer and tune my heartless breast –
                    Defer no time,
That so thy favours, granting my request,
                    They and my mind may chime
                                And mend my rhyme.   30

Dialogue

'Sweetest Saviour, if my soul
                    Were but worth the having,
Quickly should I then control
                    Any thought of waiving.
But, when all my cares and pains
Cannot give the name of gains
To thy wretch so full of stains,
What delight or hope remains?'

'What, child, is the balance thine,
                    Thine the poise and measure?   10
If I say thou shalt be mine,
                    Finger not my treasure.
What the gains in having thee
Do amount to, only he
Who for man was sold can see:
That transferred the accounts to me.'

'But, as I can see no merit
                    Leading to this favour,

So the way to fit me for it
    Is beyond my savour.   20
As the reason, then, is thine,
So the way is none of mine –
I disclaim the whole design:
Sin disclaims, and I resign.'

'That is all, if that I could
    Get without repining,
And my clay, my creature, would
    Follow my resigning.
That, as I did freely part
With my glory and desert,   30
Left all joys to feel all smart—'
    'Ah! no more – thou break'st my heart.'

Easter Wings

Lord, who created'st man in wealth and store,
    Though foolishly he lost the same,
        Decaying more and more
            Till he became
              Most poor:
              With thee
            Oh, let me rise
        As larks, harmoniously,
    And sing this day thy victories:
Then shall the fall further the flight in me.   10

My tender age in sorrow did begin,
    And still with sicknesses and shame
        Thou did'st so punish sin
            That I became
              Most thin.
              With thee

Let me combine,
And feel this day thy victory:
For if I imp my wing on thine,
Affliction shall advance the flight in me.   20

The Elixir

Teach me, my God and King,
In all things thee to see,
And what I do in anything,
To do it as for thee:

Not rudely, as a beast,
To run into an action,
But still to make thee prepossessed,
And give it his perfection.

A man that looks on glass,
On it may stay his eye,   10
Or, if he pleaseth, through it pass,
And then the heaven espy.

All may of thee partake:
Nothing can be so mean
Which, with his tincture, for thy sake,
Will not grow bright and clean.

A servant with this clause
Makes drudgery divine:
Who sweeps a room as for thy laws
Makes that, and the action, fine.   20

This is the famous stone
That turneth all to gold:

For that which God doth touch and own
Cannot for less be told.

Jordan (1)

Who says that fictions only, and false hair,
Become a verse? Is there in truth no beauty?
Is all good structure in a winding stair?
May no lines pass except they do their duty,
    Not to a true, but painted, chair?

Is it no verse, except enchanted groves
And sudden arbours shadow coarse-spun lines?
Must purling streams refresh a lover's loves?
Must all be veiled, while he that reads, divines,
    Catching the sense at two removes?   10

Shepherds are honest people: let them sing.
Riddle who list, for me, and pull for prime –
I envy no man's nightingale or spring;
Nor let them punish me with loss of rhyme
    Who plainly say: 'My God, my King'.

Life

I made a posy while the day ran by:
Here will I smell my remnant out, and tie
                    My life within this band.
But Time did beckon to the flowers, and they
By noon most cunningly did steal away,
                    And withered in my hand.

My hand was next to them, and then my heart:
I took, without more thinking, in good part
            Time's gentle admonition,
Who did so sweetly death's sad taste convey,   10
Making my mind to smell my fatal day,
            Yet sugaring the suspicion.

Farewell, dear flowers: sweetly your time ye spent,
Fit, while ye lived, for smell or ornament,
            And, after death, for cures.
I follow straight, without complaints or grief,
Since, if my scent be good, I care not if
            It be as short as yours.

Love (3)

Love bade me welcome, but my soul drew back,
            Guilty of dust and sin.
But quick-eyed Love, observing me grow slack
            From my first entrance in,
Drew nearer to me, gently questioning
            If I lacked anything.

'A guest,' I answered, 'worthy to be here':
            Love said: 'You shall be he.'
'I, the unkind, ungrateful? Ah, my dear,
            I cannot look on thee.'   10
Love took my hand, and smiling did reply:
            'Who made the eyes, but I?'

'Truth, Lord, but I have marred them: let my shame
            Go where it doth deserve.'
'And know you not,' says Love, 'who bore the blame?'
            'My dear, then I will serve.'

'You must sit down', says Love, 'and taste my meat':
          So I did sit and eat.

Mortification

How soon doth man decay!
When clothes are taken from a chest of sweets
          To swaddle infants, whose young breath
                    Scarce knows the way,
          Those clouts are little winding sheets
Which do consign and send them unto death.

          When boys go first to bed,
They step into their voluntary graves –
          Sleep binds them fast; only their breath
                    Makes them not dead: 10
          Successive nights, like rolling waves,
Convey them quickly, who are bound for death.

          When youth is frank and free,
And calls for music while his veins do swell,
          All day exchanging mirth and breath
                    In company,
          That music summons to the knell
Which shall befriend him at the house of death.

          When man grows staid and wise,
Getting a house and home, where he may move   20
          Within the circle of his breath,
                    Schooling his eyes,
          That dumb enclosure maketh love
Unto the coffin that attends his death.

          When age grows low and weak,
Marking his grave, and thawing every year,
          Till all do melt and drown his breath

When he would speak,
A chair or litter shows his bier
Which shall convey him to the house of death.   30

Man, ere he is aware,
Hath put together a solemnity,
    And dressed his hearse while he has breath
        And yet to spare:
    Yet, Lord, instruct us so to die
That all these dyings may be life in death.

Paradise

I bless thee, Lord, because I GROW
Among thy trees, which, in a ROW
To these both fruit and order   OW,

What open force, or hidden   CHARM
Can blast my fruit, or bring me HARM,
While the enclosure is thine   ARM?

Enclose me still, for fear I   START;
Be to me rather sharp and   TART,
Than let me want thy hand and ART.

When thou dost greater judgements SPARE,   10
And with thy knife but prune and   PARE
Even fruitful trees more fruitful   ARE.

Such sharpness shows the sweetest FREND;
Such cuttings rather heal than   REND;
And such beginnings touch their   END.

Peace

Sweet Peace, where dost thou dwell? I humbly crave,
    Let me once know.
  I sought thee in a secret cave,
    And asked if Peace were there:
A hollow wind did seem to answer, 'No;
    Go seek elsewhere.'

I did; and, going, did a rainbow note.
    'Surely,' thought I,
  This is the lace of Peace's coat:
    I will search out the matter.'   10
But while I looked, the clouds immediately
    Did break and scatter.

Then went I to a garden, and did spy
    A gallant flower,
  The crown imperial: 'Sure,' said I,
    'Peace at the root must dwell.'
But when I digged, I saw a worm devour
    What showed so well.

At length I met a reverend, good, old man
    Whom, when for Peace   20
  I did demand, he thus began:
    'There was a prince of old
At Salem dwelt, who lived with good increase
    Of flock and fold.

'He sweetly lived; yet sweetness did not save
    His life from foes.
  But, after death, out of his grave
    There sprang twelve stalks of wheat,
Which many, wondering at, got some of those
    To plant and set.   30

'It prospered strangely, and did soon disperse
    Through all the earth,

For they that taste it do rehearse
That virtue lies therein –
A secret virtue, bringing peace and mirth
By flight of sin.

'Take of this grain, which in my garden grows,
And grows for you.
Make bread of it: and that repose
And peace which everywhere   40
With so much earnestness you do pursue,
Is only there.'

The Pilgrimage

I travelled on, seeing the hill where lay
My expectation.
A long it was (and weary) way:
The gloomy cave of Desperation
I left on the one, and on the other side,
The rock of Pride.

And so I came to Fancy's meadow, strewed
With many a flower:
Fain would I there have make abode,
But I was quickened by my hour.   10
So to Care's copse I came, and there got through
With much ado.

That led me to the wild of Passion, which
Some call the wold –
A wasted place, but sometimes rich.
Here I was robbed of all my gold,
Save one good angel, which a friend had tied
Close to my side.

At length I got unto the gladsome hill
Where lay my hope,   20

Where lay my heart. And, climbing still,
When I had gained the brow and top,
A lake of brackish waters on the ground
                    Was all I found.

With that, abashed, and struck with many a sting
                    Of swarming fears,
          I fell, and cried: 'Alas, my King,
          Can both the way and end be tears?'
Yet, taking heart, I rose, and then perceived
                    I was deceived: 30

My hill was further. So I flung away,
                    Yet heard a cry
          Just as I went: 'None goes that way
          And lives.' 'If that be all,' said I,
'After so foul a journey death is fair,
                    And but a chair.'

The Posy

          Let wits contest,
And with their words and posies windows fill:
          'Less than the least
Of all thy mercies' is my posy still.

                    This on my ring,
This by my picture, in my book, I write:
          Whether I sing,
Or say, or dictate, this is my delight.

          Invention rest;
Comparisons go play; wit use thy will: 10

'Less than the least
Of all God's mercies' is my posy still.

Prayer (1)

Prayer: the church's banquet, angels' age,
    God's breath in man returning to his birth,
    The soul in paraphrase, heart in pilgrimage,
The Christian plummet sounding heaven and earth;

Engine against the Almighty, sinners' tower,
    Reversèd thunder, Christ-side-piercing spear,
    The six-days' world transposing in an hour,
A kind of tune which all things hear and fear;

Softness, and peace, and joy, and love, and bliss,
    Exalted manna, gladness of the best,   10
    Heaven in ordinary, man well dressed,
The Milky Way, the bird of paradise,
  Church bells beyond the stars heard, the soul's blood,
    The land of spices; something understood.

The Pulley

     When God at first made man,
Having a glass of blessings standing by,
'Let us' (said he) 'pour on him all we can:
Let the world's riches, which dispersèd lie,
     Contract into a span.'

     So strength first made a way;
Then beauty flowed, then wisdom, honour, pleasure.

When almost all was out, God made a stay,
    Perceiving that, alone of all his treasure,
        Rest in the bottom lay.   10

        'For if I should' (said he)
'Bestow this jewel also on my creature,
He would adore my gifts instead of me,
And rest in Nature, not the God of Nature:
        So both should losers be.

        'Yet let him keep the rest,
But keep them with repining restlessness:
Let him be rich and weary, that at least,
If goodness lead him not, yet weariness
        May toss him to my breast.'   20

Redemption

Having been tenant long to a rich lord,
    Not thriving, I resolvèd to be bold,
    And make a suit unto him to afford
A new, small-rented lease, and cancel the old.

In heaven at his manor I him sought:
    They told me there that he was lately gone
    About some land which he had dearly bought
Long since on earth, to take possession.

I straight returned and, knowing his great birth,
    Sought him accordingly in great resorts –   10
    In cities, theatres, gardens, parks and courts.
At length I heard a ragged noise, and mirth

    Of thieves and murderers: there I him espied,
    Who straight 'Your suit is granted' said, and died.

Sin's Round

Sorry I am, my God, sorry I am
That my offences course it in a ring.
My thoughts are working like a busy flame
Until their cockatrice they hatch and bring;
And when they once have perfected their drafts,
My words take fire from my inflamèd thoughts.

My words take fire from my inflamèd thoughts,
Which spit it forth like a Sicilian hill.
They vent the wares, and pass them with their faults,
And by their breathing ventilate the ill.   10
But words suffice not where are lewd intentions:
My hands do join to finish the inventions.

My hands do join to finish the inventions,
And so my sins ascend three storeys high,
As Babel grew before there were dissensions.
Yet ill deeds loiter not, for they supply
New thoughts of sinning: wherefore, to my shame,
Sorry I am, my God, sorry I am.

Vanity (1)

The fleet astronomer can bore
And thread the spheres with his quick-piercing mind:
He views their stations, walks from door to door,
Surveys as if he had designed
To make a purchase there. He sees their dances,
And knoweth long before
Both their full-eyed aspects and secret glances.

The nimble diver with his side
Cuts through the working waves that he may fetch

His dearly-earnèd pearl, which God did hide   10
            On purpose from the venturous wretch
That he might save his life, and also hers
            Who, with excessive pride,
Her own destruction and his danger wears.

            The subtle chemic can divest
And strip the creature naked till he find
The callow principles within their nest:
            There he imparts them to his mind,
Admitted to their bedchamber before
            They appear trim and dressed   20
To ordinary suitors at the door.

            What hath not man sought out and found
But his dear God? – who yet his glorious law
Embosoms in us, mellowing the ground
            With showers and frosts, with love and awe,
So that we need not say 'Where's this command?'
            Poor man, thou searchest round
To find out death, but missest life at hand.

Virtue

Sweet day, so cool, so calm, so bright,
The bridal of the earth and sky:
The dew shall weep thy fall tonight,
            For thou must die.

Sweet rose, whose hue angry and brave
Bids the rash gazer wipe his eye:
Thy root is ever in its grave,
            And thou must die.

Sweet spring, full of sweet days and roses,
A box where sweets compacted lie: 10

My music shows ye have your closes,
           And all must die.

Only a sweet and virtuous soul,
Like seasoned timber, never gives,
But, though the whole world turn to coal,
           Then chiefly lives.

ANDREW MARVELL

from Miscellaneous Poems (1681)

Bermudas

Where the remote Bermudas ride
In the ocean's bosom unespied,
From a small boat that rowed along
The listening winds received this song:
   'What should we do but sing his praise
That led us through the watery maze
Unto an isle so long unknown
And yet far kinder than our own,
Where he the huge sea-monsters wracks
That lift the deep upon their backs?   10
He lands us on a grassy stage,
Safe from the storms and prelate's rage.
He gave us this eternal spring,
Which here enamels everything,

And sends the fowl to us in care
On daily visits through the air.
He hangs in shades the orange bright,
Like golden lamps in a green night,
And does in pomegranates close
Jewels more rich than Ormuz shows.   20
He makes the figs our mouths to meet,
And throws the melons at our feet;
But apples plants of such a price
No tree could ever bear them twice.
With cedars, chosen by his hand
From Lebanon, he stores the land,
And makes the solemn seas that roar
Proclaim the ambergris on shore.
He cast (of which we rather boast)
The gospel's pearl upon our coast,   30
And in these rocks for us did frame
A temple, where to sound his name.
Oh, let our voice his praise exalt,
Till it arrive at heaven's vault,
Which thence (perhaps) rebounding, may
Echo beyond the Mexic bay.'
    Thus sang they, in the English boat,
An holy and a cheerful note,
And all the way, to guide their chime,
With falling oars they kept the time.   40

The Coronet

When for the thorns with which I long, too long,
    With many a piercing wound
    My Saviour's head have crowned,
I seek with garlands to redress that wrong:
    Through every garden, every mead,
I gather flowers (my fruits are only flowers),
    Dismantling all the fragrant towers

That once adorned my shepherdess's head.
And now, when I have summed up all my store,
   Thinking (so I myself deceive)   10
   So rich a chaplet thence to weave
As never yet the king of glory wore,
   Alas, I find the serpent old
   That, twining in his speckled breast,
   About the flowers disguised does fold
   With wreaths of fame and interest.
Ah, foolish man, that would'st debase with them,
And mortal glory, heaven's diadem!
But thou, who only could'st the serpent tame,
Either his slippery knots at once untie,   20
And disentangle all his winding snare,
Or shatter, too, with him my curious frame,
And let these wither so that he may die
(Though set with skill and chosen out with care)
That they, while thou on both their spoils dost tread,
May crown thy feet that could not crown thy head.

Damon the Mower

Hark how the mower, Damon, sung,
With love of Juliana stung,
While everything did seem to paint
The scene more fit for his complaint.
Like her fair eyes the day was fair,
But scorching, like his amorous care;
Sharp like his scythe his sorrow was,
And withered, like his hopes, the grass.

'Oh, what unusual heats are here,
Which thus our sunburnt meadows sear!   10
The grasshopper its pipe gives o'er,
And hamstringed frogs can dance no more;
But in the brook the green frog wades,

And grasshoppers seek out the shades:
Only the snake that, kept within,
Now glitters in its second skin.

'This heat the sun could never raise,
Nor dog-star so inflame the days:
It from an higher beauty grow'th,
Which burns the fields and mower both;   20
Which mads the dog, and makes the sun
Hotter than his own Phaëthon.
Not July causeth these extremes,
But Juliana's scorching beams.

'Tell me where I may pass the fires
Of the hot day, or hot desires:
To what cool cave shall I descend,
Or to what gelid fountain bend?
Alas, I look for ease in vain
When remedies themselves complain!   30
No moisture but my tears do rest,
Nor cold but in her icy breast.

'How long wilt thou, fair shepherdess,
Esteem me and my presents less?
To thee the harmless snake I bring,
Disarmèd of its teeth and sting;
To thee, chameleons changing hue,
And oak leaves tipped with honey dew.
Yet thou, ungrateful, hast not sought
Nor what they are, nor who them brought.   40

'I am the mower Damon, known
Through all the meadows I have mown.
On me the morn her dew distils
Before her darling daffodils,
And, if at noon my toil me heat,
The sun himself licks off my sweat,
While, going home, the evening sweet
In cowslip-water bathes my feet.

'What though the piping shepherd stock
The plains with an unnumbered flock –   50
This scythe of mine discovers wide
More ground than all his sheep do hide.
With this the golden fleece I shear
Of all these closes every year,
And, though in wool more poor than they,
Yet am I richer far in hay.

'Nor am I so deformed to sight
(If in my scythe I lookèd right,
In which I see my picture done
As, in a crescent moon, the sun).   60
The deathless fairies take me oft
To lead them in their dances soft;
And, when I tune myself to sing,
About me they contract their ring.

'How happy might I still have mowed,
Had not Love here his thistles sowed!
But now I all the day complain,
Joining my labour to my pain,
And with my scythe cut down the grass –
Yet still my grief is where it was;   70
But, when the iron blunter grows,
Sighing I whet my scythe and woes.'

While thus he threw his elbow round,
Depopulating all the ground,
And with his whistling scythe does cut
Each stroke between the earth and root,
The edgèd steel (by careless chance)
Did into his own ankle glance,
And there among the grass fell down,
By his own scythe, the mower mown.   80

'Alas,' said he, 'these hurts are slight
To those that die by Love's despite.
With shepherd's-purse and clown's-all-heal

The blood I staunch, and wound I seal;
Only for him no cure is found
Whom Juliana's eyes do wound:
'Tis Death alone that this must do,
For, Death, thou art a mower, too.'

The Garden

How vainly men themselve amaze
To win the palm, the oak, or bays,
And their uncessant labours see
Crowned from some single herb or tree
Whose short and narrow vergèd shade
Does prudently their toils upbraid,
While all flowers and all trees do close
To weave the garlands of repose.

Fair Quiet, have I found thee here,
And Innocence, thy sister dear?   10
Mistaken long, I sought you then
In busy companies of men –
Your sacred plants, if here below,
Only among the plants will grow:
Society is all but rude
To this delicious solitude.

No white nor red was ever seen
So amorous as this lovely green.
Fond lovers, cruel as their flame,
Cut in these trees their mistress' name –   20
Little, alas, they know, or heed,
How far these beauties hers exceed.
Fair trees, wheresoe'er your barks I wound,
No name shall but your own be found.

When we have run our passion's heat,
Love hither makes his best retreat.

The gods, that mortal beauty chase,
Still in a tree did end their race:
Apollo hunted Daphne so
Only that she might laurel grow,
And Pan did after Syrinx speed
Not as a nymph, but for a reed. 30

What wondrous life is this I lead!
Ripe apples drop about my head;
The luscious clusters of the vine
Upon my mouth do crush their wine;
The nectarine and curious peach
Into my hands themselves do reach;
Stumbling on melons as I pass,
Ensnared with flowers, I fall on grass. 40

Meanwhile the mind, from pleasure less,
Withdraws into it happiness:
The mind – that ocean where each kind
Does straight his own resemblance find,
Yet it creates – transcending these –
Far other worlds and other seas,
Annihilating all that's made
To a green thought in a green shade.

Here, at the fountain's sliding foot,
Or at some fruit tree's mossy root, 50
Casting the body's vest aside,
My soul into the boughs does glide:
There, like a bird, it sits and sings,
Then whets and combs its silver wings,
And, till prepared for longer flight,
Waves in its plumes the various light.

Such was that happy garden state
While man there walked without a mate:
After a place so pure and sweet,
What other help could yet be meet! 60
But 'twas beyond a mortal's share

To wander solitary there –
Two paradises 'twere in one
To live in paradise alone.

How well the skilful gardener drew
Of flowers and herbs this dial new,
Where, from above, the milder sun
Does through a fragrant zodiac run,
And, as it works, the industrious bee
Computes its time as well as we!   70
How could such sweet and wholesome hours
Be reckoned but with herbs and flowers!

An Horatian Ode upon Cromwell's Return from Ireland

The forward youth that would appear
Must now forsake his muses dear,
    Nor in the shadows sing
    His numbers languishing.
'Tis time to leave the books in dust,
And oil the unusèd armour's rust,
    Removing from the wall
    The corslet of the hall.
So restless Cromwell could not cease
In the inglorious arts of peace,   10
    But through adventurous war
    Urgèd his active star
And, like the three-forked lightning first
Breaking the clouds where it was nursed,
    Did through his own side
    His fiery way divide
(For 'tis all one to encourage high,
The emulous or enemy –
    And with such to enclose

Is more than to oppose).   20
Then burning through the air he went,
And palaces and temples rent,
    And Caesar's head at last
    Did through his laurels blast.
'Tis madness to resist or blame
The force of angry heaven's flame,
    And (if we would speak true)
    Much to the man is due,
Who, from his private gardens – where
He lived reservèd and austere,   30
    As if his highest plot
    To plant the bergamot –
Could by industrious valour climb
To ruin the great work of time,
    And cast the kingdoms old
    Into another mould,
Though Justice against Fate complain,
And plead the ancient rights in vain –
    But those do hold or break
    As men are strong or weak.   40
Nature, that hateth emptiness,
Allows of penetration less,
    And therefore must make room
    Where greater spirits come.
What fields of all the Civil Wars
Where his were not the deepest scars?
    And Hampton shows what part
    He had of wiser art,
Where, twining subtle fears with hope,
He wove a net of such a scope   50
    That Charles himself might chase
    To Carisbrooke's narrow case,
That hence the royal actor borne
The tragic scaffold might adorn,
    While around the armèd bands
    Did clap their bloody hands.
He nothing common did, or mean,
Upon that memorable scene,
    But with his keener eye

The axe's edge did try;   60
Nor called his gods with vulgar spite
To vindicate his helpless right,
    But bowed his comely head
    Down, as upon a bed.
This was that memorable hour
Which first assured the forcèd power.
    So, when they did design
    The Capitol's first line,
A bleeding head where they begun
Did fright the architects to run –   70
    And yet, in that, the state
    Foresaw its happy fate.
And now the Irish are ashamed
To see themselves in one year tamed:
    So much one man can do
    That does both act and know.
They can affirm his praises best,
And have (though overcome) confessed
    How good he is, how just,
    And fit for highest trust,   80
Nor yet grown stiffer with command,
But still in the Republic's hand:
    How fit he is to sway
    That can so well obey.
He to the Commons' feet presents
A kingdom for his first year's rents,
    And, what he may, forbears
    His fame to make it theirs,
And has his sword and spoils ungirt
To lay them at the public's skirt.   90
    So when the falcon high
    Falls heavy from the sky,
She, having killed, no more does search
But on the next green bough to perch,
    Where, when he first does lure,
    The falconer has her sure.
What may not, then, our isle presume
While victory his crest does plume?
    What may not others fear

If thus he crown each year? –
A Caesar, he, ere long, to Gaul; 100
To Italy, an Hannibal;
 And, to all states not free,
 Shall climacteric be.
The Pict no shelter now shall find
Within his particoloured mind,
 But from this valour sad
 Sink underneath the plaid,
Happy if, in the tufted brake,
The English hunter him mistake, 110
 Nor lay his hounds in near
 The Caledonian deer.
But thou – the Wars', and Fortune's, son –
March indefatigably on,
 And, for the last effect,
 Still keep thy sword erect:
Besides the force it has to fright
The spirits of the shady night,
 The same arts that did gain
 A power must it maintain. 120

The Mower against Gardens

Luxurious man, to bring, his vice in use,
 Did after him the world seduce,
And from the fields the flowers and plants allure
 Where nature was most plain and pure.
He first enclosed within the gardens square
 A dead and standing pool of air,
And a more luscious earth for them did knead,
 Which stupefied them while it fed.
The pink grew then as double as his mind –
 The nutriment did change the kind. 10
With strange perfumes he did the roses taint,
 And flowers themselves were taught to paint;

The tulip white did for complexion seek,
    And learned to interline its cheek:
Its onion root they then so high did hold
    That one was for a meadow sold.
Another world was searched, through oceans new,
    To find the 'Marvel of Peru'.
And yet these rarities might be allowed
    To man – that sovereign thing and proud –   20
Had he not dealt, between the bark and tree,
    Forbidden mixtures there to see.
No plant now knew the stock from which it came;
    He grafts upon the wild the tame
That the uncertain and adulterate fruit
    Might put the palate in dispute.
His green seraglio has its eunuchs, too
    (Lest any tyrant him outdo),
And in the cherry he does nature vex
    To procreate without a sex.   30
'Tis all enforced, the fountain and the grot,
    While the sweet fields do lie forgot,
Where willing nature does to all dispense
    A wild and fragrant innocence,
And fauns and fairies do the meadows till
    More by their presence than their skill.
Their statues, polished by some ancient hand,
    May, to adorn the gardens, stand:
But, howsoe'er the figures do excel,
    The gods themselves with us do dwell.   40

The Mower to the Glow-worms

Ye living lamps, by whose dear light
The nightingale does sit so late
And, studying all the summer night,
Her matchless songs does meditate;

Ye country comets, that portend
No war, nor prince's funeral –
Shining unto no higher end
Than to presage the grass's fall;

Ye glow-worms, whose officious flame
To wandering mowers shows the way   10
That in the night have lost their aim,
And after foolish fires do stray:

Your courteous lights in vain you waste
Since Juliana here is come,
For she my mind hath so displaced
That I shall never find my home.

The Mower's Song

My mind was once the true survey
Of all these meadows fresh and gay,
And in the greenness of the grass
Did see its hopes as in a glass –
When Juliana came, and she
What I do to the grass does to my thoughts and me.

But these, while I with sorrow pine,
Grew more luxuriant still and fine,
That not one blade of grass you spied
But had a flower on either side –   10
When Juliana came, and she
What I do to the grass does to my thoughts and me.

Unthankful meadows! – could you so
A fellowship so true forgo,
And in your gaudy May games meet
While I lay trodden under feet?

When Juliana came, and she
What I do to the grass does my thoughts and me.

But what you in compassion ought
Shall now by my revenge be wrought,   20
And flowers, and grass, and I, and all,
Will in one common ruin fall;
For Juliana comes, and she
What I do to the grass does to my thoughts and me.

And thus, ye meadows, which have been
Companions of my thoughts more green,
Shall now the heraldry become
With which I will adorn my tomb –
For Juliana comes, and she
What I do to the grass does to my thoughts and me.   30

The Nymph Complaining of the Death of her Fawn

The wanton troopers riding by
Have shot my fawn, and it will die.
Ungentle men! They cannot thrive
To kill thee! – thou never did'st alive
Them any harm: alas, nor could
Thy death yet do them any good.
I'm sure I never wished them ill,
Nor do I do all this, nor will.
But, if my simple prayers may yet
Prevail with heaven to forget   10
Thy murder, I will join my tears
Rather than fail. But – oh, my fears –
It cannot die so. Heaven's king

Keeps register of everything,
And nothing may we use in vain –
E'en beasts must be with justice slain,
Else men are made their deodands:
Though they should wash their guilty hands
In this warm lifeblood, which doth part
From thine and wound me to the heart,   20
Yet could they not be clean – their stain
Is dyed in such a purple grain
There is not such another in
The world to offer for their sin.

   Unconstant Sylvio (when yet
I had not found him counterfeit)
One morning – I remember well –
Tied in this silver chain and bell
Gave it to me. Nay, and I know
What he said then, I'm sure I do.   30
Said he: 'Look how your huntsman here
Hath caught a fawn to hunt his *dear*.'
But Sylvio soon had me beguiled –
This waxèd tame while he grew wild
And, quite regardless of my smart,
Left me his fawn but took his heart.

   Thenceforth I set myself to play
My solitary time away
With this – and, very well content,
Could do mine idle life have spent,   40
For it was full of sport, and light
Of foot and heart, and did invite
Me to its game. It seemed to bless
Itself in me: how could I less
Than love it? Oh, I cannot be
Unkind to a beast that loveth me.

   Had it lived long I do not know
Whether it, too, might have done so
As Sylvio did: his gifts might be
Perhaps as false – or more – than he.   50

But I am sure (for aught that I
Could in so short a time espy)
Thy love was far more better than
The love of false and cruel men.
  With sweetest milk and sugar first
I at mine own fingers nursed,
And, as it grew, so every day
It waxed more white and sweet than they.
It had so sweet a breath, and oft
I blushed to see its foot more soft   60
And white – shall I say, than my hand? –
Nay, any lady's of the land.
  It is a wondrous thing how fleet
'Twas on those little silver feet:
With what a pretty, skipping grace
It oft would challenge me the race;
And, when it had left me far away,
'Twould stay, and run again, and stay
(For it was nimbler much than hinds,
And trod as on the foúr winds).   70
  I have a garden of my own,
But so with roses overgrown,
And lilies, that you would it guess
To be a little wilderness;
And all the springtime of the year
It only lovèd to be there.
Amongst the beds of lilies I
Have sought it oft, where it should lie,
Yet could not – till itself would rise –
Find it, although before mine eyes,   80
For, in the flaxen lilies' shade,
It like a bank of lilies laid.
Upon the roses it would feed
Until its lips e'en seemed to bleed,
And then to me would boldly trip
And print those roses on my lip;
But its chief delight was still

On roses thus itself to fill,
And its pure virgin limbs to fold
In whitest sheets of lilies cold: 90
Had it lived long, it would have been
Lilies without, roses within.

    Oh help, oh help! I see it faint,
And die as calmly as a saint.
See how it weeps – the tears do come
Sad, slowly dropping like a gum:
So weeps the wounded balsam; so
The holy frankincense doth flow;
The brotherless Heliades
Melt in such amber tears as these.   100

    I in a golden vial will
Keep these two crystal tears, and fill
It till it do o'erflow with mine,
Then place it in Diana's shrine.

    Now my sweet fawn is vanished to
Whither the swans and turtles go –
In fair Elysium to endure,
With milk-white lambs and ermines pure.
Oh, do not run too fast, for I
Will but bespeak thy grave, and die.   110

    First my unhappy statue shall
Be cut in marble; and withal,
Let it be weeping, too (but there
The engraver sure his art may spare,
For I so truly thee bemoan
That I shall weep though I be stone),
Until my tears (still dropping) wear
My breast, themselves engraving there.
There, at my feet, shalt thou be laid,
Of purest alabaster made;   120
For I would have thine image be
White as I can – though not as thee.

On a Drop of Dew

See how the orient dew,
Shed from the bosom of the morn
    Into the blowing roses,
Yet careless of its mansion new,
For the clear region where 'twas born
    Round in itself encloses,
    And, in its little globe's extent,
Frames as it can its native element.
    How it the purple flower does slight,
        Scarce touching where it lies,   10
    But, gazing back upon the skies,
        Shines with a mournful light,
            Like its own tear,
Because so long divided from the sphere.
    Restless it rolls, and unsecure,
        Trembling lest it grow impure,
    Till the warm sun pity its pain
And to the skies exhale it back again.
    So the soul – that drop, that ray
Of the clear fountain of eternal day –   .   20
Could it within the human flower be seen,
    Remembering still its former height,
    Shuns the sweet leaves and blossoms green
    And, recollecting its own light,
Does – in its pure and circling thoughts – express
The greater heaven in an heaven less.
    In how coy a figure wound
    Every way it turns away,
    So the world excluding round,
    Yet receiving in the day,   30
    Dark beneath, but bright above,
    Here disdaining, there in love.
    How loose and easy thence to go,
    How girt and ready to ascend:
    Moving but on a point below
    It all about does upwards bend.
Such did the manna's sacred dew distil,

White and entire, though congealèd and chill –
Congealèd on earth, but does, dissolving, run
Into the glories of the almighty sun.   40

To His Coy Mistress

Had we but world enough, and time,
This coyness, lady, were no crime:
We would sit down, and think which way
To walk, and pass our long love's day:
Thou by the Indian Ganges' side
Should'st rubies find; I by the tide
Of Humber would complain. I would
Love you ten years before the Flood,
And you should (if you please) refuse
Till the conversion of the Jews.   10
My vegetable love should grow
Vaster than empires, and more slow:
An hundred years should go to praise
Thine eyes, and on thy forehead gaze;
Two hundred to adore each breast
(But thirty thousand to the rest);
An age (at least) to every part,
And the last age should show your heart:
For, lady, you deserve this state,
Nor would I love at lower rate.   20
      But, at my back, I always hear
Time's wingèd chariot hurrying near
And, yonder, all before us lie
Deserts of vast eternity:
Thy beauty shall no more be found,
Nor, in thy marble vault, shall sound
My echoing song. Then worms shall try
That long-preserved virginity,
And your quaint honour turn to dust –

And, into ashes, all my lust.   30
The grave's a fine and private place –
But none, I think, do there embrace.
    Now, therefore – while the youthful glue
Sits on thy skin like morning dew,
And while thy willing soul transpires
At every pore with instant fires –
Now let us sport us while we may,
And now – like amorous birds of prey –
Rather at once our time devour
Than languish in his slow-chapped power.   40
Let us roll all our strength and all
Our sweetness up into one ball,
And tear our pleasures with rough strife
Through the iron gates of life.
Thus – though we cannot make our sun
Stand still – yet we will make him run.

from Upon Appleton House:
To My Lord Fairfax

(LINES 481–592)

But I, retiring from the flood,
Take sanctuary in the wood
And, while it lasts, myself embark
In this yet green, yet growing, ark,
Where the first carpenter might best
Fit timber for his keel have pressed,
And where all creatures might have shares
(Although in armies, not in pairs).

The double wood of ancient stocks,
Linked in so thick, an union locks: 490
It like two pedigrees appears,
On the one hand Fairfax, the other, Vere's –
Of whom, though many fell in war,
Yet more to heaven shooting are
And, as they Nature's cradle decked,
Will, in green age, her hearse expect.

When first the eye this forest sees,
It seems, indeed, as wood not trees,
As if their neighbourhood so old
To one great trunk them all did mould.   500
There the huge bulk takes place, as meant
To thrust up a fifth element,
And stretches still, so closely wedged
As if the night within were hedged.

Dark all without it knits: within
It opens passable and thin,
And in as loose an order grows
As the Corinithian porticoes;
The arching boughs unite between
The columns of the temple green   510
And, underneath, the wingèd choirs
Echo about their tunèd fires.

The nightingale does here make choice
To sing the trials of her voice:
Low shrubs she sits in, and adorns
With music high the squatted thorns;
But highest oaks stoop down to hear,
And listening elders prick the ear.
The thorn – lest it should hurt her – draws
Within the skin its shrunken claws.   520

But I have, for my music, found
A sadder, yet more pleasing, sound:
The stock-doves, whose fair necks are graced
With nuptial rings, their ensigns chaste –

Yet always, for some cause unknown,
Sad pair, unto the elms they moan.
Oh, why should such a couple mourn,
That in so equal flames do burn?

Then as I, careless, on the bed
Of gelid strawberries do tread,   530
And through the hazels thick espy
The hatching throstle's shining eye,
The heron from the ash's top
The eldest of its young lets drop,
As if it, stork-like, did pretend
That tribute to its lord to send.

But most the hewel's wonders are,
Who here has the holtfelster's care:
He walks still upright from the root,
Measuring the timber with his foot,   540
And all the way – to keep it clean –
Doth from the bark the woodmoths glean.
He, with his beak, examines well
Which fit to stand and which to fell.

The good he numbers up and hacks,
As if he marked them with the axe:
But where he, tinkling with his beak,
Does find the hollow oak to speak,
That for his building he designs,
And through the tainted side he mines.   550
Who could have thought the tallest oak
Should fall by such a feeble stroke!

Nor would it, had the tree not fed
A traitor worm, within it bred
(As first our flesh, corrupt within,
Tempts impotent and bashful sin).
And yet that worm triumphs not long,
But serves to feed the hewel's young –
While the oak seems to fall content,
Viewing the treason's punishment.   560

Thus I, easy philospher,
Among the birds and trees confer,
And little now to make me wants
Or of the fowls or of the plants:
Give me but wings as they, and I
Straight floating on the air shall fly;
Or turn me but, and you shall see
I was but an inverted tree.

Already I begin to call
In their most learned original   570
And, where I language want, my signs
The bird upon the bough divines,
And more attentive there doth sit
Than if she were with lime-twigs knit:
No leaf does tremble in the wind
Which I, returning, cannot find.

Out of these scattered sibyl's leaves
Strange prophecies my fancy weaves,
And in one history consumes,
Like Mexic paintings, all the plumes.   580
What Rome, Greece, Palestine ere said,
I, in this light mosaic, read:
Thrice-happy he who, not mistook,
Hath read in Nature's mystic book.

And see how Chance's better wit
Could, with a mask, my studies hit:
The oak leaves me embroider all,
Between which caterpillars crawl,
And ivy, with familiar trails,
Me licks, and clasps, and curls, and hales.   590
Under this antic cope I move
Like some great prelate of the grove.

HENRY VAUGHAN

from Silex Scintillans: or, Sacred Poems and Private Ejaculations (1650)

Corruption

Sure, it was so. Man in those early days
      Was not all stone and earth:
He shined a little, and by those weak rays
      Had some glimpse of his birth.
He saw heaven o'er his head, and knew from whence
      He came (condemnèd) hither,
And, as first love draws strongest, so from hence
      His mind sure progressed thither.
Things here were strange unto him: sweat and till –
      All was a thorn, or weed;   10
Nor did those last, but (like himself) died still.
      As soon as they did seed
They seemed to quarrel with him, for that act
      That felled him, foiled them all:
He drew the curse upon the world, and cracked
      The whole frame with his fall.
This made him long for home, as loath to stay
      With murmurers and foes:
He sighed for Eden, and would often say
      'Ah, what bright days were those!'   20
Nor was heaven cold unto him, for each day
      The valley or the mountain
Afforded visits, and still paradise lay
      In some green shade or fountain.
Angels lay ledger here: each bush and cell,
      Each oak and highway knew them –

Walk but the fields, or sit down at some well,
　　　And he was sure to view them.
Almighty Love, where art thou now? Mad man
　　　Sits down and freezeth on:　　　　　　　　30
He raves, and swears to stir nor fire nor fan,
　　　But bids the thread be spun.
I see thy curtains are close-drawn; thy bow
　　　Looks dim, too, in the cloud.
Sin triumphs still, and man is sunk below
　　　The centre, and his shroud:
All's in deep sleep and night; thick darkness lies
　　　And hatcheth o'er thy people.
But hark! What trumpet's that? What angel cries
　　　'Arise! Thrust in thy sickle'?　　　　　　40

The Dawning

Ah, what time wilt thou come? When shall that cry
　　　'The bridegroom's coming!' fill the sky?
Shall it in the evening run
When our words and work are done,
　　　Or will thy all-surprising light
　　　　Break at midnight,
When either sleep or some dark pleasure
Possesseth mad man without measure?
Or shall these early, fragrant hours
　　　Unlock thy bowers,　　　　　　　　10
And with their blush of light descry
Thy locks crowned with eternity?
Indeed, it is the only time
That with thy glory doth best chime.
All now are stirring; every field
　　　Full hymns doth yield;
The whole creation shakes off night,
And forth thy shadow looks the light;

Stars now vanish without number;
Sleepy planets set and slumber;   20
The pursy clouds disband and scatter –
All expect some sudden matter;
Not one beam triumphs, but from far
      That morning star.

Oh, at what time soever thou,
Unknown to us, the heavens wilt bow
And, with thy angels in the van,
Descend to judge poor, careless man,
Grant I may not like puddle lie
In a corrupt security,   30
Where, if a traveller water crave,
He finds it dead and in a grave;
But – as this restless, vocal spring
All day and night doth run and sing,
And (though here born) yet is acquainted –
Elsewhere and, flowing, keeps untainted –
So let me all my busy age
In thy free services engage,
And though (while here) of force I must
Have commerce, sometimes, with poor dust,   40
And in my flesh – though vile and low –
As this doth in her channel, flow,
Yet, let my course, my aim, my love,
And chief acquaintance be above,
So when that day and hour shall come
In which thyself will be the Sun,
Thou'lt find me dressed and on my way,
Watching the break of thy great day.

'I walked the other day'

I walked the other day (to spend my hour)
      Into a field
Where I sometimes had seen the soil to yield
      A gallant flower;

But winter now had ruffled all the bower
        And curious store
     I knew there heretofore.

Yet I – whose search loved not to peep and peer
        I'the face of things –
Thought with myself, there might be other springs   10
        Besides this here
Which, like cold friends, sees us but once a year,
        And so the flower
     Might have some other bower.

Then, taking up what I could nearest spy,
        I digged about
That place where I had seen him to grow out,
        And by and by
I saw the warm recluse alone to lie
        Where, fresh and green,   20
     He lived of us unseen.

Many a question intricate and rare
        Did I there strew,
But all I could extort was that he now
        Did there repair
Such losses as befell him in this air,
        And would, ere long,
     Come forth most fair and young.

This past, I threw the clothes quite o'er his head
        And, stung with fear   30
Of my own frailty, dropped down many a tear
        Upon his bed,
Then, sighing, whispered 'Happy are the dead.
        What peace doth now
     Rock him asleep below!'

And yet, how few believe such doctrine springs
        From a poor root
Which, all the winter, sleeps here under foot,
        And hath no wings

To raise it to the truth and light of things,   40
        But is still trod
    By every wandering clod.

O thou, whose spirit did at first inflame
        And warm the dead,
And by a sacred incubation fed
        With life this frame
Which once had neither being, form, nor name:
        Grant I may so
    Thy steps track here below

That in these masks and shadows I may see   50
        Thy sacred way,
And by those hid ascents climb to that day
        Which breaks from thee,
Who art in all things – though invisibly.
        Show me thy peace,
    Thy mercy, love and ease,

And from this care, where dreams and sorrows reign,
        Lead me above
Where light, joy, leisure and true comforts move
        Without all pain.   60
There, hid in thee, show me his life again
        At whose dumb urn
    Thus all the year I mourn.

Peace

    My soul, there is a country
        Far beyond the stars,
    Where stands a wingèd sentry
        All skilful in the wars:
    There, above noise and danger,
        Sweet Peace sits crowned with smiles,

And one born in a manger
    Commands the beauteous files.
He is thy gracious friend,
    And – oh, my soul, awake –   10
Did in pure love descend
    To die here for thy sake.
If thou canst get but thither,
    There grows the flower of peace –
The rose that cannot wither,
Thy fortress and thy ease.
Leave, then, thy foolish ranges,
    For none can thee secure
But one who never changes –
    They God, thy life, thy cure.   20

Retirement (1)

Who on yon throne of azure sits,
    Keeping close house
Above the morning star –
    Whose meaner shows
And outward utensils these glories are
    That shine, and share
Part of his mansion – he, one day,
    When I went quite astray,
      Out of mere love,
      By his mild dove,   10
Did show me home, and put me in the way.

'Let it suffice at length thy fits
    And lusts' (said he)
    'Have had their wish and way:
    Press not to be
Still thy own foe, and mine; for to this day
    I did delay,
    And would not see, but chose to wink –

Nay, at the very brink
    And edge of all,   20
        When thou would'st fall,
My love-twist held thee up, my unseen link.

'I know thee well, for I have framed,
    And hate thee not.
        Thy spirit, too, is mine:
            I know thy lot,
Extent and end, for my hands drew the line
    Assignèd thine.
        If, then, thou would'st unto my seat,
            'Tis not the applause, and feet   30
                Of dust and clay
                Leads to that way,
But from those follies a resolved retreat.

'Now, here below (where, yet untamed,
    Thou dost thus rove),
        I have a house, as well
            As there above.
In it my name and honour both do dwell,
    And shall, until
        I make all new. There's nothing gay   40
            In perfumes or array –
                Dust lies with dust,
                And hath but just
The same respect, and room, with every clay:

'A faithful school, where thou may'st see,
    In heraldry
        Of stones and speechless earth,
            Thy true descent;
Where dead men preach, who can turn feasts and mirth
    To funerals and Lent.   50
        There dust, that out of doors might fill
            Thy eyes, and blind thee still,
                Is fast asleep:
                Up, then, and keep
Within those doors – my doors. Dost hear?' 'I will.'

The Retreat

Happy those early days, when I
Shined in my angel infancy –
Before I understood this place
Appointed for my second race,
Or taught my soul to fancy aught
But a white, celestial thought;
When yet I had not walked above
A mile or two from my first love
And, looking back (at that short space),
Could see a glimpse of his bright face;   10
When on some gilded cloud or flower
My gazing soul would dwell an hour,
And in those weaker glories spy
Some shadows of eternity;
Before I taught my tongue to wound
My conscience with a sinful sound,
Or had the black art to dispense
A several sin to every sense,
But felt through all this fleshly dress
Bright shoots of everlastingness.   20
    Oh, how I long to travel back,
And tread again that ancient track,
That I might once more reach that plain
Where first I left my glorious train,
From whence the enlightened spirit sees
That shady city of palm trees!
But – ah – my soul with too much stay
Is drunk, and staggers in the way.
Some men a forward action love,
But I by backward steps would move,   30
And, when this dust falls to the urn,
In that state I came, return.

The Shower

'Twas so — I saw thy birth. That drowsy lake
From her faint bosom breathed thee, the disease
Of her sick waters and infectious ease.
       But now, at even,
       Too gross for heaven,
Thou fall'st in tears and weep'st for thy mistake.

Ah, it is so with me: oft have I pressed
Heaven with a lazy breath but, fruitless, this
Pierced not. Love only can, with quick access,
       Unlock the way   10
       When all else stray
The smoke, and exhalations of the breast.

Yet if, as thou dost melt and, with thy train
Of drops, make soft the earth, my eyes could weep
O'er my hard heart that's bound up and asleep,
       Perhaps at last,
       Some such showers past,
My God would give a sunshine after rain.

'Silence, and stealth of days'

Silence, and stealth of days! 'Tis now,
       Since thou art gone,
Twelve hundred hours, and not a brow
       But clouds hang on.
As he that, in some cave's thick damp,
       Locked from the light,
Fixeth a solitary lamp
       To brave the night
And, walking from his sun, when past
       That glimmering ray,   10

Cuts through the heavy mists in haste
    Back to his day,
So, o'er fled minutes, I retreat
    Unto that hour
Which showed thee last, but did defeat
    Thy light and power.
I search, and rack my soul to see
    Those beams again,
But nothing but the snuff to me
    Appeareth plain: 20
That, dark and dead, sleeps in its known
    And common urn,
But those fled to their Maker's throne
    There shine and burn.
Oh, could I track them! But souls must
    Track one the other,
And now the spirit, not the dust,
    Must be my brother.
Yet I have one pearl, by whose light
    All things I see,
And in the heart of earth and night   30
    Find heaven, and thee.

Son-days

Bright shadows of true rest; some shoots of bliss;
                Heaven once a week;
The next world's gladness prepossessed in this;
                A day to seek
Eternity in time; the steps by which
We climb above all ages; lamps that light
Man through his heap of dark days; and the rich
And full redemption of the whole week's flight.

The pulleys unto headlong man; time's bower;
                The narrow way;   10

Transplanted paradise; God's walking hour;
     The cool o' the day;
The creatures' jubilee; God's parle with dust;
Heaven here; man on those hills of myrrh and flowers;
Angels descending; the returns of trust;
A gleam of glory after six-days-showers.

The church's love-feasts; time's prerogative
     And interest
Deducted from the whole; the combs, and hive,
     And home of rest;   20
The Milky Way, chalked out with suns; a clue
That guides through erring hours and, in full story,
A taste of heaven on earth; the pledge and cue
Of a full feast; and the out-courts of glory.

The World (1)

I saw eternity the other night,
Like a great ring of pure and endless light,
    All calm as it was bright;
And, round beneath it, time in hours, days, years,
     Driven by the spheres,
Like a vast shadow moved, in which the world
     And all her train were hurled.
The doting lover in his quaintest strain
     Did there complain –
Near him his lute, his fancy, and his flights   10
     (Wit's sour delights),
With gloves and knots, the silly snares of pleasure
     (Yet his dear treasure)
All scattered lay, while he his eyes did pour
     Upon a flower.

The darksome statesman, hung with weights and woe,
Like a thick midnight fog moved there so slow

He did not stay nor go:
Condemning thoughts like sad eclipses scowl
       Upon his soul,
And clouds of crying witnesses without
       Pursued him with one shout.
Yet digged the mole, and, lest his ways be found,
       Worked under ground,
Where he did clutch his prey: but one did see
       That policy.
Churches and altars fed him; perjuries
       Were gnats and flies;
It rained about him blood and tears, but he
       Drank them as free.

The fearful miser on a heap of rust
(Sat pining all his life there) did scarce trust
       His own hands with the dust,
Yet would not place one piece above, but lives
       In fear of thieves.
Thousands there were as frantic as himself,
       And hugged, each one, his pelf:
The downright epicure placed heaven in sense
       And scorned pretence,
While others (slipped into a wide excess)
       Said little less.
The weaker sort slight, trivial wares enslave
       Who think them brave,
And poor, despisèd Truth sat counting by
       Their victory.

Yet some – who, all this while, did weep and sing,
And sing and weep – soared up into the ring;
       But most would use no wing.
'Oh, fools,' said I, 'thus to prefer dark night
       Before true light;
To live in grots and caves, and hate the day
       Because it shows the way –
The way which from this dead and dark abode
       Leads up to God;
A way where you might tread the sun and be

More bright than he.'
But, as I did their madness so discuss,
    One whispered thus:
'This ring the bridegroom did for none provide
    But for his bride.'   60

                John 2:16–17
All that is in the world, the lust of the flesh, the lust of the eyes,
and the pride of life, is not of the father, but is of the world.
    And the world passeth away, and the lusts thereof, but he that
doth the will of God abideth for ever.

Vanity of Spirit

Quite spent with thoughts I left my cell, and lay
Where a shrill spring tuned to the early day.
    I begged here long, and groaned to know
    Who gave the clouds so brave a bow,
    Who bent the spheres, and circled in
    Corruption with this glorious ring –
    What is his name, and how I might
    Descry some part of his great light.
I summoned Nature, pierced through all her store,
Broke up some seals which none had touched before: 10
    Her womb, her bosom and her head
    (Where all her secrets lay abed)
    I rifled quite, and, having passed
    Through all her creatures, came at last
    To search myself, where I did find
    Traces and sounds of a strange kind.
Here, of this mighty spring, I found some drills,
With echoes beaten from the eternal hills:
    Weak beams and fires flashed to my sight
    Like a young east or moonshine night,   20
    Which showed me, in a nook cast by,

A piece of much antiquity,
With hieroglyphics quite dismembered,
And broken letters scarce remembered.
I took them up and, much joyed, went about
T'unite those pieces, hoping to find out
          The mystery; but, this near done,
          That little light I had was gone.
          It grieved me much. At last said I:
          'Since in these veils my eclipsèd eye   30
          May not approach thee (for at night
          Who can have commerce with the light?),
          I'll disapparel, and – to buy
          But one half glance – most gladly die.'

from **Silex Scintillans, Part 2** (1655)

Childhood

I cannot reach it, and my striving eye
Dazzles at it as at eternity.
          Were now that chronicle alive –
Those white designs which children drive,
And the thoughts of each harmless hour,
With their content, too, in my power –
Quickly would I make my path even
And, by mere playing, go to heaven.

          Why should men love
A wolf more than a lamb or dove,   10
Or choose hell-fire and brimstone streams
Before bright stars and God's own beams?
Who kisseth thorns will hurt his face,

But flowers do both refresh and grace
And, sweetly living (fie on men!),
Are, when dead, medicinal then.
If seeing much should make staid eyes,
And long experience should make wise,
Since all that age doth teach is ill,
Why should I not love childhood still?   20
Why, if I see a rock or shelf,
Should I from thence cast down myself,
Or, by complying with the world,
From the same precipice be hurled?
Those observations are but foul
Which make me wise to lose my soul.

And yet the practice worldlings call
Business and weighty action all,
Checking the poor child for his play,
But gravely cast themselves away.   30

      Dear, harmless age – the short, swift span
Where weeping virtue parts with man;
Where love without lust dwells, and bends
What way we please without self-ends.

An age of mysteries, which he
Must live twice that would God's face see;
Which angels guard, and with it play –
Angels, which foul men drive away!

How do I study now, and scan
Thee more than e'er I studied man,   40
And only see through a long night
Thy edges and thy bordering light!
Oh for thy centre and midday,
For sure that is the 'narrow way'.

Cock crowing

Father of lights, what sunny seed,
What glanced of day, hast thou confined
Into this bird? To all the breed
This busy ray thou hast assigned:
   Their magnetism works all night,
   And dreams of paradise and light.

Their eyes watch for the morning hue,
Their little grain, expelling night,
So shines and sings as if it knew
The path unto the house of light.   10
   It seems their candle, howe'er done,
   Was teened and lighted at the sun.

If such a tincture, such a touch,
So firm a longing can empower,
Shall thy own image think it much
To watch for thy appearing hour?
   If a mere blast so fill the sail,
   Shall not the breath of God prevail?

O, thou immortal light and heat,
Whose hand so shines through all this frame   20
That, by the beauty of the seat,
We plainly see who made the same! –
   Seeing thy seed abides in me,
   Dwell thou in it, and I in thee.

To sleep without thee is to die –
Yes, 'tis a death partakes of hell;
For where thou dost not close the eye,
It never opens, I can tell:
   In such a dark, Egyptian border
   The shades of death dwell, and disorder.   30

If joys, and hopes, and earnest throes,
And hearts, whose pulse beats still for light,

Are given to birds, who (but thee) knows
A lovesick soul's exalted flight?
   Can souls be tracked by an eye
   But his, who gave them wings to fly?

Only this veil, which thou hast broke,
And must be broken yet in me –
This veil, I say – is all the cloak
And cloud which shadows thee from me.   40
   This veil thy full-eyed love denies,
   And only gleams and fractions spies.

Oh, take it off, make no delay,
But brush me with thy light that I
May shine unto a perfect day,
And warm me at thy glorious eye!
   Oh, take it off – or, till it flee,
   Though with no lily, stay with me!

The Night (John 3:2)

   Through that pure virgin shrine –
That sacred veil drawn o'er thy glorious noon
That men might look and live as glow-worms shine,
   And face the moon –
   Wise Nicodemus saw such light
   As made him know his God by night.

   Most blest believer he
Who, in that land of darkness and blind eyes,
Thy long-expected healing wings could see
   When thou did'st rise,   10
   And – what can never more be done –
   Did at midnight speak with the sun!

Oh, who will tell me where
He found thee at that dead and silent hour?
What hallowed, solitary ground did bear
    So rare a flower,
     Within whose sacred leaves did lie
     The fullness of the deity?

     No mercy-seat of gold,
No dead and dusty cherub, nor carved stone,   20
But his own living works did my Lord hold
    And lodge alone,
     Where trees and herbs did watch, and peep,
     And wonder, while the Jews did sleep.

    Dear night! – this world's defeat;
The stop to busy fools; care's check and curb;
The day of spirits; my soul's calm retreat
    Which none disturb;
     Christ's progress and his prayer time;
     The hours to which high heaven doth chime;   30

    God's silent, searching flight,
When my Lord's head is filled with dew, and all
His locks are wet with the clear drops of night;
    His still, soft call;
     His knocking time; the soul's dumb watch
     When spirits their fair kindred catch:

    Were all my loud, evil days
Calm and unhaunted as is thy dark tent,
Whose peace (but by some angel's wing or voice)
    Is seldom rent,
                         40
     Then I in heaven all the long year
     Would keep, and never wander here.

    But, living where the sun
Doth all things wake, and where all mix and tire
Themselves and others, I consent and run
    To every mire,

And by this world's ill-guiding light
Err more than I can do by night.

There is in God (some say)
A deep but dazzling darkness – as men here   50
Say 'it is late and dusky' because they
See not all clear:
Oh for that night when I in him
Might live invisible and dim!

'They are all gone into the world of light'

They are all gone into the world of light,
And I alone sit lingering here;
Their memory is fair and bright,
And my sad thoughts doth clear:

It glows and glitters in my cloudy breast
Like stars upon some gloomy grove,
Or those faint beams in which this hill is dressed
After the sun's remove.

I see them walking in an air of glory
Whose light doth trample on my days –   10
My days which are at best but dull and hoary,
Mere glimmerings and decays.

O holy Hope and high Humility –
High as the heavens above!
These are your walks, and you have showed them me
To kindle my cold love,

Dear, beauteous Death – the jewel of the just,
Shining nowhere but in the dark.
What mysteries do lie beyond thy dust,
Could man outlook that mark!   20

He that hath found some fledged bird's nest may know
    At first sight if the bird be flown –
But what fair well or grove he sings in now,
    That is to him unknown.

And yet, as angels in some brighter dreams
    Call to the soul when man doth sleep,
So some strange throughts transcend our wonted themes,
    And into glory peep.

If a star were confined into a tomb,
    Her captive flames must need burn there;   30
But when the hand that locked her up gives room,
    She'll shine through all the sphere.

O father of eternal life and all
    Created glories under thee,
Resume thy spirit from this world of thrall
    Into true liberty:

Either disperse these mists which blot and fill
    My perspective still as they pass;
Or else remove me hence unto that hill
    Where I shall need no glass.   40

The Waterfall

What deep murmurs through Time's silent stealth
Doth thy transparent, cool and watery wealth
    Here flowing fall,
    And chide and call,
As if his liquid, loose retinue stayed
Lingering and were of this steep place afraid –
    The common pass
    Where, clear as glass,
    All must descend:

                        Not to an end,   10
       But, quickened by this deep and rocky grave,
       Rise to a longer course more bright and brave.
                    Dear stream, dear bank, where often I
                    Have sat and pleased my pensive eye,
                    Why (since each drop of thy quick store
                    Runs hither, whence it flowed before)
                    Should poor souls fear a shade or night
                    Who came (sure) from a sea of light?
                    Or, since those drops are all sent back
                    So sure to thee (that none doth lack),   20
                    Why should frail flesh doubt any more
                    That what God takes he'll not restore?
                    O useful element and clear –
                    My sacred wash and cleanser here;
                    My first consigner unto those
                    Fountains of life where the Lamb goes! –
                    What sublime truths and wholesome themes
                    Lodge in thy mystical, deep streams!
                    Such as dull man can never find
                    Unless that Spirit lead his mind   30
                    Which first upon thy face did move
                    And hatched all with his quickening love.
                    As this loud brook's incessant fall
                    In steaming rings restagnates all
                    Which reach, by course, the bank, and then
                    Are no more seen, just so pass men.
                    O, my invisible estate,
                    My glorious liberty, still late:
                    Thou art the channel my soul seeks –
                    Not this with cataracts and creeks!   40

Notes

NOTE: spelling and punctuation have been modernised in all texts.

Donne

Text: unless otherwise stated, from *Poems, by J.D. With Elegies on the Author's Death* (1633), where most of his poetry was first published.

Songs and Sonnets

The Apparition **1 scorn ... dead:** courtly love posture. Literary antecedents include Wyatt, 'My lute, awake!' **5 vestal:** virgin (after the virgin guardians of the Roman temple of Vesta, goddess of fire, who kept the temple lamps burning). **6 sick taper:** emblem of approaching death (also: guttering vestal lamp); **wink:** flicker; go out. **11 aspen:** shivering; from asp (*populus tremula*), associated with death. **12 quicksilver:** mercury (silver, hence dedicated to the moon goddess of virginity); mobile, hence emblem of inconstancy. **17 innocent:** unharmed.

The Canonisation **title:** formal admission into the calendar of saints. **4 state:** material prosperity. **5 Take ... course:** aim at self-advancement; **place:** at court. **6 Observe ... Grace:** cultivate a nobleman or bishop. **7 real:** regal; actual; small Spanish silver coin. **8 approve:** attempt. **11–14 sighs ... heats:** traditional (Petrarchan) lovers' afflictions. **15 plaguey bill:** weekly list of plague victims. **17 move:** provoke. **20 fly:** moth, consumed by **taper** flame as lovers are by lust. **21 die:** come to orgasm (believed to shorten life). **22 eagle:** heavenly power; masculine; **dove:** celestial purity; female. **23 phoenix:** unique androgynous bird fabled to regenerate itself from its own ashes. **26 the same:** unharmed. **27 Mysterious:** i.e., a truth known only by revelation. **29 hearse:** metal framework over tomb. **30 legend:** saints' life; inscription. **32 rooms:** puns on Italian *stanza* = room, apartment. **39 rage:** ardour; divine possession. **40 contract:** concentrate. **41 glasses ... eyes:** cf. *The Good Morrow*, 15 (also: the eye is window to the soul).

The Dream common topic after Ovid, *Amores*, 1.5; and cf. Spenser, *Fairy*

Queen, 1.1.46–55. **4 fantasy:** imagination. **25 brave:** also, splendid.
27–8 torches . . . out: one previously lit is more easily reignited.

The Flea   erotic flea poems were common after the pseudo-Ovidian 'Song
of the Flea'. **4 flea . . . be:** 'mingling blood' = sexual intercourse.

The Good Morrow   3 country pleasures: coarse sexual fun; the
suckling of an infant by a rustic wet-nurse. **4 seven . . . den:** legend has
it that when the Roman emperor Decius persecuted the Christians in A.D.
249–50, seven noble Ephasian youths took refuge in a cave; they woke
after two centuries. **13 maps:** of the heavens. **18 north:** destructive,
evil; **west:** death. **19 dies . . . equally:** man's pre-Fall body consisted of
an exact balance of the four elements.

Love's Alchemy   7 chemic: alchemist; **elixir:** the philosophers' stone
(which transmutes base matter to gold); the panacea bestowing
immortality. **22 minstrelsy:** wedding music, especially outside bridal
chamber door; **spheres:** ancient belief that each planet revolved on a
sphere, which produced a musical note. **24 mummy:** dead flesh;
possessed: when sexually penetrated; controlled by a demon (as false
Florimell: Spenser, *Fairy Queen*, 3.8).

Love's Growth   1 pure: unmixed, hence unaffected by change.
7–8 cures . . . more: the ancient idea that like cures like; **quintes-
sence:** purest (heavenly) essence, superior to the four elements.
14 Love . . . do: the Christian 'mixed' life of contemplation and action.
23 spheres: the concentric planetary spheres.

A Nocturnal . . .   title Nocturnal: night-piece; a *nocturn* was a division
of the midnight office of matins; **St Lucy's Day:** 13 December; thought
of as the shortest day, though not the winter solstice (then, 12
December), when the sun enters the zodiacal sign of Capricorn (the **Goat**
of **40**). Donne's patroness, **Lucy**, Countess of Bedford, was ill 1612/13;
Lucy means light; **St Lucy**, virgin martyr, patroness of sight, died A.D.
304. **1 midnight:** solstice. **3 flasks:** the stars, containers of his light;
flickering rays. **6 general balm:** innate preservative of life; **hydroptic:**
over-thirsty. **15 quintessence:** its distillation or extraction
(**14 express**) from the four elements was a main goal of alchemy.
21 limbeck: alchemical retort. **29 elixir:** essence offering long life
and freedom from disease; the philosophers' stone. **31 prefer:** choose
(we are endowed with choice by the sensitive soul, shared by man and
beasts). **33 stones:** thought able to attract and repel. **36 As:** such as.

The Primrose   (1635 subtitle: 'being at Montgomery Castle [seat of the
Herbert family], upon the hill on which it is situate'.) **4 manna:**
heavenly dew (food for Israelites: Exodus 16); yellow drops from manna-

ash, etc. **8 true love:** in folklore, a six- or four-petalled flower, but often identified with the primrose, which has **five (22)**, the number of marriage because the product of two (female) + three (male). **23 women:** the primrose was often associated with maidens. **25 Ten: farthest** because all subsequent numbers merely reduplicate the first ten and because it is celestial (the number of the heavenly spheres); Donne identifies it, as the number of perfection and the rational soul (P. Bongus, *Numerorum mysteria* (Bergamo, 1599), pp. 362–3, 573), with man.

The Relic **3 womanhead:** womanhood. **6 bright:** fair. **13 misdevotion:** prayers to saints (rather than God). **17 Mary Magdalen:** the penitent whore, said to be the lover of Christ. **21 paper:** i.e., poem. **22 harmless:** innocent. **30 late law:** human laws, result of the Fall.

Song (*'Go, and catch . . .'*) **2 mandrake:** plant with forked root thought to scream when dug up. **6 stinging:** from Envy's emblematic snakes.

Song (*'Sweetest love . . .'*) **34 Forethink:** presage; plan.

The Sun Rising **8 country ants:** industrious farmers; **offices:** duties. **17 Indias:** the East Indies for spice; the West for gold. **24 alchemy:** i.e., illusion.

The Undertaking **2 Worthies:** nine great warriors from Hector to Geoffrey of Boulogne. **6 specular stone:** transparent stone needing great skill to cut it thinly.

A Valediction **9 Moving:** i.e., earthquakes. **11 trepidation:** oscillation. **12 innocent:** harmless. **13 sublunary:** earthly, mortal. **17 refined:** purified (beyond the four **elements**). **26 stiff:** stable; **compasses:** emblem of constancy.

Woman's Constancy **14 scapes:** tricks; sallies of wit.

From *An Anatomy* text 1633 (first printed 1611). Elegy for the young Elizabeth Drury, imagining her as embodied perfection without whom the world collapses. **205 new philosophy:** of Copernicus, Galileo, etc., describing a heliocentric universe to displace the geocentric Ptolemaic one. **206 fire:** the old view was that the earth was surrounded by water, air and fire, then the planetary spheres. **217 phoenix:** *see The Canonisation*, 23n. **221–6 She . . . way:** links her with Virgin Mary as star of the sea. **230 Gilt . . . East:** see *The Sun Rising*, 17n. **234 single money:** small change. **243 hectic:** wasting.

Divine Meditations
Sonnet 5 Text: *Poems* (1635 edn). **1 little world:** microcosm, of **elemental** matter and **spirit** (see *The Good Morrow*, 19n.). **5 You:** astronomers; the blessed dead. **9–10 Or . . . burnt:** Genesis 9:11; Malachi 4:1. **14 eating:** Holy Communion.

Sonnet 6 (1633) **13 Impute:** Protestant doctrine of inherited guilt from Adam which can be erased only by the grace which imputes Christ's righteousness to believers (Anglican Articles of Religion, 9–11). **14 world . . . devil:** baptism rite in Book of Common Prayer.

Sonnet 7 (1633) **1 corners:** on maps; also Revelation 7:1 (for **corners** and **angels**). **7–9 you . . . sleep:** 1 Corinthians 15:51–5.

Sonnet 9 (1633) **1 tree:** Genesis 2–3. The named things **cannot be damned** because they lack free will. **11 Lethean:** Lethe was the river of forgetfulness in Hades.

Sonnet 10 (1633) **4 Die . . . me:** see ***Sonnet 7***. 7–9n. **12 swell'st:** with pride.

Sonnet 13 (1633) **5 amazing:** terrifying. **7 adjudge:** sentence. **8 Which . . . spite:** Luke 23:34. **14 assures:** guarantees.

Sonnet 14 (1633) **9 fain:** willingly. **11 knot:** sign of marriage (here, to the devil). **14 ravish:** in the Platonic sense of seizure of the soul by a god (and cf. 2 Corinthians 12:2–4).

Sonnet 17 (Westmoreland MS; printed E. Gosse, *Jacobean Poets*, 1894). Donne's wife died in 1617. **6 head:** source (God: Jeremiah 2:13, etc.) **8 melts:** moves. **10 thine:** i.e., Christ as dowry. **14 put . . . out:** expel; outdo.

A Hymn to Christ . . . the visit lasted from May 1619 to January 1620. **2 ark:** Genesis 6–8; an emblem of baptism (1 Peter 3:20–1). **15 root:** Christ (Isaiah 11:1, 10). **17 control:** restrain. **21 from . . . more:** from abundance of love. **22 takes:** gains; seizes.

Hymn to God . . . text: 1635. Possibly written shortly before his death; but he had been seriously ill in December 1623. **3 thy music:** one of your musicians; part of your harmony. **9 south-west:** i.e., hot (not the north-west passage). **10 Per . . . febris:** through the strait (also: violent heat) of fever; **straits:** also: difficulties. **11 west:** death. **13 east:** Christ. **14 In . . . one:** when rolled into a cylinder. **16 Pacific:** peaceful. **17 eastern riches:** Christ; wealth of Cathay; **Jerusalem:** means 'vision of peace'. **18 Anyan:** channel thought to divide America from Asia (now Annam). **20 Japhet . . . Shem:** Noah's three sons; they received Europe, Africa and Asia respectively. **21–2 We . . . place:** paradise was agreed to have been in Mesopotamia, not too far from Jerusalem. **25 last Adam:** Christ. **26 purple:** blood; robe of crucifixion (John 19).

Herbert

Text: The Temple. Sacred Poems and Private Ejaculations (1633).

Superliminare **title:** above the lintel (Latin). The poem is placed between the first part of *The Temple*, 'The Church Porch' (the **former precepts** of **1**) and the main body of poems, entitled 'The Church'. **2 Sprinkled:** with holy water. **4 repast:** Communion. **5 Avoid:** depart (cf. *Aeneid*, 6.258: 'Hence, uninitiated ones [*profani*]').

Aaron **title:** Moses' brother, type of the true priest; his garments are described in Exodus 28: the mitre, inscribed 'Holiness to the Lord', is on the **head** (**1**); the **breastplate** contains the Urim (= **Light**) and Thummim (= **perfection**); the robe's hem is decorated with gold **bells** (**3**). **8 noise:** band of musicians. **16 Christ . . . head:** 1 Corinthians 11:3. **18–19 dead . . . man:** Romans 6:6 (death of our **old man** – Adam, sin – with Christ).

The Altar **3 frame:** shape (for **heart** (**2**) not **stone** (**6**) see 2 Corinthians 3:3). **4 No . . . same:** Exodus 20:25. **11 frame:** structure (poem).

Anagram . . . John 1:14 (where 'dwelt' means 'pitched his tent'); Song of Solomon 6:4

The Church Floor **10 in . . . band:** Colossians 3:14. **14 neat:** elegant; **curious:** delicate.

Church Monuments **8 elements:** letters; and cf. ***The Good Morrow***, 19n. **9 lines:** also, ancestral. **20 glass:** hour glass.

The Collar **title:** an emblem of discipline, possibly also clerical; chain; choler (yellow bile, bodily fluid believed to cause anger). And cf. Job 30:11,18. **1 board:** table; Communion table. **5 store:** plenty. **6 still . . . suit:** ever dancing attendance. **9 cordial:** reviving; for/from the heart. **14 bays:** laurels. **15 blasted:** blighted. **22 rope of sands:** imagined difficulties (proverb). **26 wink:** close your eye.

Dialogue **4 waiving:** refusing your offer. **10 poise:** balance. **20 savour:** value; understanding. **22 way:** John 14:6. **31 smart:** grief; wounds.

Easter Wings For the wings, see Malachi 4:2. **10 fall . . . me:** the Augustinian notion that Adam's fall (Genesis 3) was fortunate because it led to Christ's redemption of man. **19 imp:** repair wing by engrafting new feathers.

The Elixir **title:** see ***Love's Alchemy***, 7n; it was also identified with Christ. **7 make . . . prepossessed:** give you prior claim. **8 his:** its. **9 glass:** 1 Corinthians 13:12. **15 tincture:** alchemical term for spiritual principle which can be infused into matter. **23 touch:** test and mark gold for purity. **24 told:** counted.

Jordan (1)   **title:** the site of Christ's baptism; baptism in general; the Jews crossed the River Jordan to reach the Promised Land. **5 chair:** earthly royal throne. **7 shadow:** conceal bad quality of. **12 list:** wants to; **pull . . . prime:** draw for winning hand in card game primero.

Life   **1 posy:** nosegay; poem (poesy); motto.

Love (3)   The last poem of 'The Church'. **3 quick:** sharp, bright (celestial, not blindfold, Cupid); **slack:** slow. **17 meat:** meal (the heavenly Communion of Luke 12:37).

Mortification   **title:** the process of dying. **2 sweets:** perfumes. **5 clouts:** swaddling clothes. **17 knell:** the passing bell (rung while one was dying). **24 attends:** awaits. **33 hearse:** decorative framework over coffin or tomb.

Paradise   **7 Enclose:** 'paradise' derives from the Persian/Greek for enclosure, park.

Peace   **15 crown imperial:** fritillaria imperialis (emblem of power). **22 prince:** Melchizedek, type of Christ as priest (Genesis 14:18), king of Salem (= peace: Hebrews 7:2). **28 stalks:** the apostles. **33 rehearse:** tell. **34 virtue:** special power. **37 Take . . . grain:** 'Take, eat' (1 Corinthians 11:24; Last Supper/Holy Communion).

The Pilgrimage   **10 hour:** life's brevity. **14 wold:** moor. **17 angel:** gold coin; guardian angel. **36 chair:** sedan-chair (comfortable way of arriving).

The Posy   **title:** see *Life*, 1n.

Prayer (1)   **banquet:** dessert; something eaten between main meals. **5 Engine:** weapon. **10 manna:** see *The Primrose*, 4n. **11 ordinary:** its own right; devotional manual; daily meal.

The Pulley   Reverses Pandora's box of human ills. **5 span:** hand width; human life.

Sin's Round   **title: Round:** repetitive canon (musical); vicious circle. **2 course it:** chase round. **4 cockatrice:** fabled cock-serpent with fatal breath. **8 Sicilian hill:** Etna, where the Cyclopes laboured as smiths. **9 vent:** discharge; utter; vend. **10 ventilate:** increase; agitate; publicise; give vent to. **15 Babel:** tower of sin (Genesis 11).

Vanity (1)   **2 spheres:** see *Love's Alchemy*, 22n. **3 stations:** apparent standings still. **7 aspects:** faces; oppositions to each other (astrology). **11 venturous:** adventurous. **15 chemic:** alchemist. **17 callow:** featherless; essential.

Virtue   **2 bridal:** wedding. **3 fall:** nightfall; cadence. **5 brave:** also, splendid. **10 sweets:** perfumes; sounds (music box). **11 closes:** cadences. **15 coal:** cinder (Day of Judgement: cf. Donne, *Sonnet 5*, 9–10n.).

Marvell

Text: Miscellaneous Poems (1681).

Bermudas   The islands were a refuge for puritans. **7 unknown:** Juan Bermudez discovered them in 1515. **9 sea-monsters:** grounded whales. **17 orange:** emblem of chastity; identified as the golden fruit of the western Garden of the Hesperides. **19 pomegranates:** decorate the Temple (2 Chronicles 3:16). **20 Ormuz:** Hormuz on Persian Gulf. **21 figs:** with **pomegranates**, in Canaan (Numbers 13:23). **22 melons:** not those of Egypt (Numbers 11:5). **23 apples:** pineapples; as in Eden. **25 cedars:** used for the Temple. **28 ambergris:** secretion of sperm whale, used in perfumery. **30 pearl:** Matthew 13:45–6.

The Coronet   **1 long:** also, desire. **7 towers:** head-dresses. **14 twining in:** entwining. **22 curious frame:** intricate structure. **25 spoils:** of victory; slough of snake.

Damon the Mower   For the tradition, see Theocritus, *Idylls*, 11; Virgil, *Eclogues*, 2. **9 heats:** hot season. **18 dog-star:** Sirius, in Canis Major, supposed to cause extreme heat and fevers with the dog days (late July to August). **22 Phaëthon:** son of Apollo, set the world on fire when he stole the sun's chariot. **48 cowslip-water:** used to ease the skin. **54 closes:** enclosed fields. **83 With . . . heal:** both (*bursa pastoris, stachys*) heal wounds (W. Salmon, *New London Dispensatory* (1678), pp. 39, 106).

The Garden   **1 amaze:** perplex; madden. **2 palm . . . bays:** the first two for military and civic achievement; the third (laurel) for poetry. **5 vergèd:** limited; extended. **6 upbraid:** censure; braid up (in linked leaves of garland). **7 close:** join. **15–16 rude/To:** uncivil compared to. **17 white . . . red:** colours traditionally used to describe the beloved's complexion. **18 amorous:** lovely. **19 Fond:** foolish; besotted. **25 run . . . heat:** run its course; exhausted its ardour. **29–32 Apollo . . . reed: Apollo**, god of sun and poetry, pursued the daughter of the River Peneus, who became a laurel; **Pan**, shepherd god and musician, chased **Syrinx**, who was turned into reeds (the pan pipe, emblem of pastoral verse). **37 curious:** delicate. **44 straight:** at once (the belief that the ocean contains the equivalents of land creatures and plants was common; refers to the power of the imagination). **47–8 Annihilating . . . To:** reducing the created world to nothing compared to. **49 sliding:** flowing; steeply sloping. **51 vest:** covering (the **bird** symbolises the soul). **54 whets:** preens. **57–8 Such . . . mate:** Eden (until, at Genesis 2:18, God creates 'an **help meet** [suitable] for' Adam). **61 share:** lot. **66 dial:** sundial.

An Horatian Ode . . .   Oliver Cromwell's punitive Irish campaign lasted from July 1649 to May 1650. **1 forward:** zealous; presumptuous; **appear:** become public. **4 numbers languishing:** love verse (cf. Virgil, *Eclogue* 1, Tityrus singing love poems in the shade). **9 cease:** rest. **15 own side:** rival parliamentary leaders. **19–20 enclose . . . more:** contain is more satisfying. **23 Caesar's:** Charles I's (lightning traditionally avoids **laurel**). **32 bergamot:** 'the pear of kings' (Cromwell had been a wheat farmer; note pun on **plot**). **41–2 Nature . . . less:** Nature abhors a vacuum, and two bodies occupying the same space. **47–52 And . . . case:** Charles fled from Hampton Court to Carisbrooke Castle on the Isle of Wight in November 1647. He was executed at Whitehall 30 January 1649; **case:** enclosure; grave. **62 To . . . right:** Divine Right. **67–70 So . . . run:** the head dug up by the builders of the temple of Jupiter on the Capitoline Hill was taken as an omen of Rome's greatness. **83 sway:** govern. **101–2:** Julius **Caesar** conquered Gaul; **Hannibal** invaded Italy. **104 climacteric:** epoch-making; fatal. **105–6 Pict . . . mind:** he invaded Scotland on 22 July 1650; **particoloured:** factious; painted (Latin *pictus*); also, the plaid. **107 sad:** weary (the Picts); firm (the 'valour'). **111 lay . . . in:** put on the scent of. **117–18 Besides . . . night:** a sword terrifies spirits (*Aeneid*, 6.260); here, the war dead, and the king.

The Mower against Gardens **1 Luxurious:** voluptuous; **in use:** into a custom. **7 luscious:** sickly; wanton. **15–16 Its . . . sold:** a tulip bulb sold in Holland for 5,500 florins. **18 'Marvel of Peru':** *Mirabilis Jalapa*. **21–2 Had . . . see:** grafting; and Deuteronomy 22:9.

The Mower to the Glow-worms **9 officious:** obliging; dutiful. **12 foolish fires:** love; will-o'-the-wisps (*ignis fatuus*).

The Mower's Song **1 survey:** view; image. **3 greenness:** colour of hope. **19 ought:** owed.

The Nymph Complaining . . . In a tradition of laments for pets (e.g., Catullus, 1.3). **1 troopers:** cavalrymen in Scottish Covenanting Army which invaded England in 1640. **17 deodands:** given up to God to atone for the murder. **22 Is . . . grain:** so utterly bloody. **71–92 I . . . within:** echoing Song of Solomon, 2, 5 and 6 (beloved (Christ) as hart feeding among lilies, etc.). **99 Heliades:** Phaëthon's (*Damon the Mower*, 22n.) sisters, turned into weeping poplars when he died. **104 Diana:** hunting goddess of chastity. **106 swans:** Cycnus, kin to Phaëthon and the Heliades, lamented their deaths and was turned into a swan; **turtles** (turtledoves) traditionally grieve for their dead mates. **108 lambs:** purity and sacrifice; **ermines:** chastity.

On a Drop of Dew **1 orient:** shining; eastern. **3 blowing:** blooming.

4 mansion: resting place; body enclosing soul. **5 For:** in place of. **14 sphere:** crystalline sphere of heaven. **24 recollecting:** collecting together; remembering its divine origins (Platonism). **27 coy:** still; secluded. **37 manna:** see *The Primrose*, 4n.

To His Coy Mistress   in the *carpe diem* (seize the day) tradition. **1 world:** life. **2 coyness:** reluctance; shyness. **4 love's day:** day for meeting and amicably settling disagreements. **8 Flood:** Genesis 7–8 (supposedly 1656 *anno mundi*). **10 Till ... Jews:** millenarian sign; Cromwell discussed the readmission of the Jews in 1655–6. **11 vegetable:** having faculty of growth. **29 quaint:** fastidious; pudenda. **33 glue:** balm (see Donne, *A Nocturnal ...* 6n.). **40 slow-chapped:** slowly-devouring (chap = jaw); slowly splitting our skin. **44 iron:** strong but fallen and subject to time (the Iron Age after the Gold, Silver, and Bronze Ages).

Upon Appleton House ... **title:** Lord General Thomas Fairfax resigned as Commander-in-Chief of the Parliamentary army in 1650 and retired to the family home, Nun Appleton in Yorkshire; Marvell was his daughter's tutor there from late 1650–2. The poem traces the house's history and considers the topic of withdrawal versus public obligation. **485 carpenter:** Noah (Genesis 6, 7). **486 pressed:** forced into service. **489–90 The ... locks:** the avenue of trees joins at one point. **491 pedigrees:** family trees. **492 Vere:** Fairfax's wife, Anne Vere. **496 hearse:** see Donne, *The Canonisation*, 29n.; **expect:** await. **499 neighbourhood:** nearness. **502 fifth element:** see Donne, *Love's Growth* 7–8n. **508 Corinthian:** this architectural order symbolised marriage: Vitruvius, *Ten Books on Architecture*, 4.1.8–10. **517 oaks:** emblems of kingship. **518 elders:** the tree; ancestors; presbyters. **523 stock-doves:** emblems of marital fidelity. **580 gelid:** cold. **535–6 As ... send:** storks were reputed to leave one of their young as a tribute to the owner of the house where they had nested. **537 hewel:** green woodpecker. **538 holtfelster:** wood-cutter. **551–2 Who ... stroke:** recalling Charles I's execution (30 January 1649). **555 corrupt:** since the Fall. **565–6 Give ... fly:** see *The Garden*, 51n. **568 an ... tree:** Plato, *Timaeus*, 90 and later writers. **571 want:** lack. **577 Out ... leaves:** the sibyl of Cumae prophesied from scattered leaves. **580 Mexic paintings:** feather pictures. **582 mosaic:** dappled floor; the Mosaic Pentateuch. **586 mask:** disguise; the court masque fashionable under James I and Charles I; **hit:** suit.

Vaughan

Text: Silex Scintillans ('The Sparking Flint'; 1650, 1655).

from *Silex Scintillans* (1650)

Corruption   cf. *The Retreat.* Based on the Fall of man (Genesis 2, 3) and
the Platonic and neo-Platonic idea of the soul's memory of its divine
origins. **2   earth:** Adam (Genesis 2:7). **9–10   sweat . . . weed:** Genesis
3:18–19; **till:** ploughing. **13   that act:** eating the forbidden fruit.
16   frame: structure. **25   ledger:** as ambassadors; also 'leaguer' =
encamped; **cell:** cave. **31   stir . . . fan:** i.e., not to stir or fan
the fires of lust **32   thread:** of life. **33   curtains:** Psalm 104:2; **bow:**
Genesis 9:13–15. **36   centre:** earth. **38   hatcheth o'er:** brings to
maturity; shades. **39–40   What . . . sickle:** Revelation 14:18 (apoca-
lyptic mowing of infidel).

The Dawning   2   The . . . coming: Matthew 25:6 (midnight). **9–10
Or . . . bowers:** see the sun-bridegroom of Psalm 19:4–5. **14   chime:**
harmonise. **21   pursy:** heavy. **24   morning star:** Christ (Revelation
22:16). **29   puddle:** polluted water. **46   Sun:** Malachi 4:1–3.

'I walked . . .'   4   A . . . flower: see Herbert, *Peace,* 13–15. **6   curious:**
skilfully wrought; **store:** abundance. **22   rare:** excellent. **29   quite:**
completely. **33   Happy . . . dead:** Revelation 14:13. **37   root:** see
Donne, *A Hymn to Christ . . .,* 15n. **45   incubation:** Genesis 1:2
('spirit' as dove; also alchemical and Hermetic). **49   Thy . . . below:** in
Nature's book (see Marvell, *Upon Appleton House . . .,* 584).
50   masks: see *Upon Appleton House . . .,* 586n. **52   ascents:** the
ladder of creation. **61   hid in thee:** Colossians 3:3; **his:** his brother
William died in July 1648.

Peace   3–4   Where . . . wars: Revelation 12:7 (battle against Satan);
contrast to the Civil War.

Retirement (1)   5   utensils: also: sacred vessels in a church. **10   dove:**
Holy Spirit. **11   put . . . way:** directed me. **22   twist:** cord. **23
framed:** formed you. **26   lot:** fate. **38   In . . . dwell:** Psalm 26:8. **40   I
. . . new:** Revelation 21:5. **45–8   A . . . descent:** see Herbert, *Church
Monuments,* 6–11.

The Retreat   title: withdrawal; period of meditative seclusion. **4   second
race:** Hebrews 12:1 (race against sin). **6   white:** innocent; auspicious.
20   shoots: of growth; swift motions. **26   That . . . trees:** Deuteron-
omy 34:1–4 (Jericho in the promised land).

The Shower   1   lake: cf. Spenser, *Fairy Queen,* 2.6 (Idle Lake). **11   stray:**
scatters.

'Silence, and stealth . . .' **3 Twelve . . . hours:** remembers William (see **'I walked . . .'**, 61n.); also the fifty days between Christ's burial and Pentecost (Acts 2:1–4). **5 cave:** Plato's cave of spiritual ignorance (*Republic*, 7). **7 lamp:** the soul; spiritual readiness (Matthew 25:1–13). **19 snuff:** burnt part of candle wick (life as taper: see Donne, *The Apparition*, 6n.). **29 pearl:** the gospel (see Marvell, *Bermudas*, 30n.)

Son-days **1 shadows:** anticipations. **3 prepossessed:** possessed beforehand. **10 narrow way:** Matthew 7:14. **11–12 God's . . . day:** Genesis 3:8. **13 jubilee:** celebration; liberty (Leviticus 25:8–13); **parle:** talk. **17 love-feasts:** Communion; **prerogative:** God-given privilege. **21 clue:** thread through maze. **24 out:** outer.

The World (1) **5 spheres:** planetary; and see Plato, *Timaeus*, 37. **7 hurled:** whirled. **12 gloves:** a common fetish; **knots:** love-knots. **14 pour:** study; cry. **25–6 one . . . policy:** God detects the Machiavellian. **28 gnats . . . flies:** mere irritations. **43 brave:** splendid. **51 caves:** see **'Silence, and stealth'**, 5n. **60 bride:** Matthew 25:1–13; Revelation 21:2.

Vanity of Spirit **title:** Ecclesiastes 1:14. **1 Quite:** utterly. **4 bow:** see **Corruption**, 33n. **17 drills:** streams. **25 joyed:** rejoicing. **33 disapparel:** undress (Song of Solomon 5:3; 2 Corinthians 5:1–4).

from *Silex Scintillans*, Part 2 (1655)

Childhood **4 white:** see **The Retreat**, 6n. **14–16 But . . . then:** see Herbert, **Life**, 13–15. **36 live . . . see:** John 3:3. **44 narrow way:** see **Son-days**, 10n.

Cock Crowing **title:** the cock is solar in Hermetic/alchemical thought; also signifies spiritual illumination. **2 glance:** brightness; bright metallic ore. **12 teened:** kindled. **13 tincture:** Herbert, **The Elixir**, 15n. **16 appearing hour:** Matthew 25:13. **20 frame:** universe (Romans 1:20). **29 Egyptian:** land of captivity (Exodus 10:21–3). **34 A . . . flight:** see Marvell, **The Garden**, 51n. **48 lily:** purity; faithful soul (Song of Solomon, 2:2,16).

The Night **title:** Nicodemus the rabbi came to Jesus by night. **1 virgin shrine:** sky containing Diana, virgin moon goddess; Christ's body. **2 veil:** Hebrews 10:20. **9 expected:** awaited; **healing wings:** Malachi 4:2. **19–20 No . . . cherub:** Exodus 25:17–22. **29 Christ's . . . time:** Vaughan supplies a reference to Mark 1:35; Luke 21:37. **32–4 When . . . call:** Song of Solomon 5:2 (also for **knocking, 35**). **38 tent:** tabernacle.

'They are all gone . . .' **10 trample on:** travels over. **20 outlook:** see beyond. **32 sphere:** the heavens. **35 Resume:** take back to yourself. **38 perspective:** spy-glass, telescope.

The Waterfall **11 quickened:** made faster; made alive. **12 brave:** splendid. **15 store:** plenty. **24 sacred wash:** baptism. **26 Fountains . . . goes:** Revelation 7:17 (the Lamb is Christ). **30–2 Spirit . . . love:** see *'I walked . . .'*, 45n. **34 restagnates:** overflows (Latinism); remains stagnant. **35 by course:** in succession. **38 glorious liberty:** Romans 8:21.

Everyman's Poetry

William Blake
ed. Peter Butter
0 460 87800 X

The Brontës
ed. Pamela Norris
0 460 87864 6

Rupert Brooke & Wilfred Owen
ed. George Walter
0 460 87801 8

Robert Burns
ed. Donald Low
0 460 87814 X

Lord Byron
ed. Jane Stabler
0 460 87810 7

John Clare
ed. R. K. R. Thornton
0 460 87823 9

Samuel Taylor Coleridge
ed. John Beer
0 460 87826 3

Four Metaphysical Poets
ed. Douglas Brooks-Davies
0 460 87857 3

Oliver Goldsmith
ed. Robert L. Mack
0 460 87827 1

Thomas Gray
ed. Robert Mack
0 460 87805 0

Ivor Gurney
ed. George Walter
0 460 87797 6

Heinrich Heine
ed. T. J. Reed & David Cram
0 460 87865 4

George Herbert
ed. D. J. Enright
0 460 87795 X

Robert Herrick
ed. Douglas Brooks-Davies
0 460 87799 2

John Keats
ed. Nicholas Roe
0 460 87808 5

Henry Wadsworth Longfellow
ed. Anthony Thwaite
0 460 87821 2

Andrew Marvell
ed. Gordon Campbell
0 460 87812 3

John Milton
ed. Gordon Campbell
0 460 87813 1

Edgar Allan Poe
ed. Richard Gray
0 460 87804 2

Poetry Please!
Foreword by Charles Causley
0 460 87824 7

Alexander Pope
ed. Douglas Brooks-Davies
0 460 87798 4

Alexander Pushkin
ed. A. D. P. Briggs
0 460 87862 X

Lord Rochester
ed. Paddy Lyons
0 460 87819 0

Christina Rossetti
ed. Jan Marsh
0 460 87820 4

William Shakespeare
ed. Martin Dodsworth
0 460 87815 8

John Skelton
ed. Greg Walker
0 460 87796 8

Alfred, Lord Tennyson
ed. Michael Baron
0 460 87802 6

R. S. Thomas
ed. Anthony Thwaite
0 460 87811 5

Walt Whitman
ed. Ellman Crasnow
0 460 87825 5

Oscar Wilde
ed. Robert Mighall
0 460 87803 4